No Congregation
Is an Island

No Congregation
Is an Island

How Faith Communities
Navigate Opportunities
and Challenges Together

Jennifer M. McClure Haraway

AN ALBAN BOOK
ROWMAN & LITTLEFIELD
Lanham • Boulder • New York • London

Published by Rowman & Littlefield
An imprint of The Rowman & Littlefield Publishing Group, Inc.
4501 Forbes Boulevard, Suite 200, Lanham, Maryland 20706
www.rowman.com

86-90 Paul Street, London EC2A 4NE

British Library Cataloguing in Publication Information Available

Library of Congress Cataloging-in-Publication Data on File

ISBN 978-1-5381-8046-4 (cloth : alk. Paper)
ISBN 978-1-5381-8047-1 (pbk. : alk. Paper)
ISBN 978-1-5381-8048-8 (electronic)

∞™ The paper used in this publication meets the minimum requirements of American
National Standard for Information Sciences—Permanence of Paper for Printed Library
Materials, ANSI/NISO Z39.48-1992.

With gratitude to Don and Pam McClure, Megan and Patrick Kamler, and Robert Haraway for your love and support

Contents

Acknowledgments

First and foremost, I am grateful to the congregational ministers and leaders who participated in this project. Thank you for trusting me with information about your congregation's relationships, opportunities, and challenges. I am honored to share your stories in this book.

I would like to thank a variety of colleagues in sociology and in related fields that study religion. I'm very grateful to you, Roger Finke, for your guidance and mentoring during graduate school, for supporting my interest in congregations, and for your help brainstorming and reframing this book to its current form. Thank you, Diane Felmlee, for training me in and nurturing my love of social network analysis and for your advice and support throughout this project. I am grateful to Sean Everton for encouraging social network analysis within sociology of religion and for the small but growing number of scholars who have used social network analysis to study congregational life: Sun Kyong Lee, Heewon Kim, and Cameron W. Piercy; Nathan R. Todd, Emily J. Blevins, and Jacqueline Yi; Katie E. Corcoran, Rachel E. Stein, Corey J. Colyer, and Brittany M. Kowalski; Mark Chapman, and Mark Killian. Thank you to Nathaniel Porter for your encouragement and support and for reading and providing feedback on many of the articles from this project that I cite in this book and to Erica Dollhopf for your friendship, encouragement, and support. I would also like to thank the colleagues who gave me feedback on the book proposal and on a variety of publishers: Roger Finke, Nancy Ammerman, Scott Thumma, Warren Bird, Sean Everton, Kathleen Cahalan, Scott Cormode, Todd Ferguson, and Tim Shapiro.

I could not have done this project without support from Samford University's Center for Congregational Resources. Michael Wilson, Keri Burno, Kelly Adams, Julia Bradley, and Abigail Ratliff, I am grateful for your support and encouragement. Thank you for brainstorming with me, for believing in me even when I wasn't sure this would work out, for your financial support of the project, for providing course releases from our Lilly Endowment grants to give me more time to work on this project, for helping to print and mail questionnaires, for providing incentives to congregational ministers and leaders who participated, and for so many other things. Keri, thanks especially for our walks around campus, for listening to my ideas, and for supporting me. I am also grateful to Samford University for a faculty development grant that partially funded this project and for a sabbatical that provided time to write this book.

Many thanks to my colleagues in Samford's Department of Biblical and Religious Studies and Department of Geography and Sociology and to the leaders of these departments—Roy Ciampa, Jennifer Speights-Binet, and Theresa Davidson. I am grateful for your help, encouragement, support, and advice. Jeff Leonard, I'm sorry for that year when we were in adjoining offices with very little soundproofing and you heard thousands of my phone calls. Thanks for being so gracious throughout the situation. Lisa Battaglia, thank you for listening to and encouraging me on our many walks and hikes. Hugh Floyd, thanks for stopping by my office to check on my progress with surveying congregations. Jennifer Rahn, Jonathan Fleming, and Jordan Cissell, thanks for showing me how to use and create maps in ArcGIS. Jonathan Fleming, thanks for making sure that the figures in this book have the necessary dimensions and clarity for printing.

I am grateful to my editor, Richard Brown; the leadership of Alban at Duke Divinity; and the four anonymous reviewers of the book proposal. Thank you for your excitement about and support for the book. Richard, thank you for your feedback about the book's content and tone and for your guidance throughout the process. You've strengthened this book and made it more useful to congregations and their ministers and leaders.

Many thanks to Abby Hogelin, Julianne Sandberg, Matt Dorning, Alexis Pappas, and Neal and Finley Evans. I am grateful for your friendship, support, encouragement, and excitement about this book.

Most of all, I would like to thank my family for their love, support, prayers, and encouragement. Thanks for listening as I thought through the book and the stories I wanted to share. Patrick, thanks for reading some chapters and providing feedback from a pastor's perspective. Mom, Dad, Megan, Patrick, and Robert, I love you.

Preface

If you're a congregational minister or leader, your congregation is undoubtedly experiencing a variety of opportunities and challenges. How you respond is largely shaped by the relationships you have with the other congregations around you. As you build trust and cooperation, you can gain access to information and resources, and all of that impacts the extent to which you can adapt and innovate.

Many faith traditions have affirmed the benefits of relationships when people engage in them responsibly. For example, in *No Man Is an Island*, theologian Thomas Merton wrote:

> Every other [hu]man is a piece of myself, for I am a part and a member of [hu]mankind. Every Christian is part of my own body, because we are members of Christ. What I do is also done for them and with them and by them. What they do is done in me and by me and for me. But each of us remains responsible for his [or her] own share in the life of the body.[1]

Although Merton was speaking about relationships among individuals, his insights apply to relationships among religious congregations as well—no congregation is an island.

In the research for this book, I spoke with fifty ministers from nineteen denominations and traditions, and many ministers readily acknowledged this fact. One minister said,

> I believe that *no [hu]man or no ministry is an island* and that we are supposed to be connected in some kind of way, . . . and I believe that in order for us to really truly impact our community, our region, [and] this nation, then each church has a different mission, and that, when all those missions can somehow be connected and be on one accord, then we can truly make a difference.

Using the language of not being an island is not coincidental because I shared the title for this book with the ministers I talked with. However, it was clear that this language resonated with them.

Another minister mentioned the numerous partnerships for community service that his Baptist congregation has been able to develop with local churches, nonprofits, businesses, and denominational associations and that have allowed his congregation to address needs for food, medical care, and housing in its community. He said,

> We are making those kind of connections, partnering with other groups, and so to your point *no church is an island*, . . . our church, believe it or not, as small as we are and as kind of insignificant as we are in the larger scheme of things, we're like a church that doesn't have a whole lot of tools, but [these connections have] propelled us into a place within the context of [our city] where our church has become a leader in helping other churches to make connections that they could not, would not have made.

For this congregation, building relationships with other congregations, ministries, and organizations has allowed it to encourage and nurture relationships between other congregations despite having fewer attenders and resources.

In addition, a minister of a predominantly African American congregation shared how relationships with other congregations have strengthened his church's impact in the community.

> I think we're stronger together. We can make a greater impact through demonstrating unity and compassion, so we're doing things actually within the community now where a number of churches are coming together to pray in various places, to have prayer walks, to have unity days, to go out and evangelize communities, to provide needs and gift cards, or to help people financially. So we're doing these things together, and it appears to me that pastors are excited about it, so we just believe that we are called to work together and *not be an island* to ourselves.

Relationships with other congregations have expanded this congregation's opportunities to minister in the community and to meet a wider variety of needs.

There are numerous ways that relationships between congregations have helped congregations to navigate opportunities and challenges, which will only increase in the years ahead. I share many of these stories in this book.

Chapter 1

Why Relationships between Congregations Matter

In difficult times, relationships can provide tangible help, advice, resources, and emotional support. This is true not just for people but also for religious congregations. U.S. congregations are experiencing many opportunities and challenges because of changes in the American religious landscape, the COVID-19 pandemic, and the increasing political and policy divisiveness. Relationships with other congregations impact how congregations are responding to the opportunities and challenges that they face.

If you're a minister or leader who's feeling stressed, overwhelmed, and perhaps bewildered by all of the changes that have taken place in congregational ministry in recent years, this book is for you. I want this book to be a resource for you about how to find support, ideas, and collaborations through relationships with other ministers, leaders, and congregations.[1]

In this book, I explore the ways in which relationships between congregations help congregations to navigate opportunities and challenges, and I draw on conversations with congregational ministers and leaders from central Alabama to share stories about five types of relationships:

- relationships primarily within religious groups
- relationships exclusively within distinctive religious groups
- relationships between religious groups
- relationships within racial groups
- relationships between racial groups

My goal is to give you numerous examples of ways that congregations can use these types of relationships to navigate changes together, to help you to understand the advantages and disadvantages of each relationship type, and to provide practical guidance about how congregations in a variety of contexts can build and utilize these relationships.

In this chapter, I provide an overview of some of the challenges and opportunities facing congregations, why relationships matter for congregations as well as their ministers and leaders, what to expect in the rest of the book as we explore the five types of relationships mentioned above, and this book's central Alabama focus and wider applicability.

CHALLENGES AND OPPORTUNITIES

Congregations are navigating many changes in the American religious landscape that are creating both challenges and opportunities for ministry. If, for you, the first and biggest change that comes to mind is the disruption from the COVID-19 pandemic, I wouldn't be surprised. However, I'll discuss the challenges and opportunities related to the pandemic last in order to highlight important changes that were taking place well before 2020. Throughout this section, you might notice that many challenges and opportunities are closely tied together.

A key challenge and opportunity facing congregations is a decline in religiosity among U.S. adults. In a 2021 Pew Research survey, about 30 percent of American adults reported no religious affiliation, and a similar percentage of adults reported never attending worship services. Some might be tempted to assume that many of these people who are not religious are opposed to religion. However, many people who are not religious are not atheist, agnostic, or antagonistic toward religion; most are just not interested in it. Some congregations see this change as an opportunity for evangelism and outreach to lead nonreligious people to develop religious commitments. However, a particular challenge for congregations is that the vast majority of religious "nones" are not looking to join a religious group.[2] Congregations seeking to grow and to recruit new attenders who are not already part of a faith community are more likely to encounter people who are not only irreligious but also not interested in being part of their congregation.

A challenge and an opportunity closely tied to the decline in religiosity involves reaching and engaging young adults. Young adults are more likely to be nonreligious than older generations, with about 40 percent of millennials being unaffiliated with religion. Young adults also attend religious services less frequently than older generations, with only 35 percent of millennials attending religious services at least once a month. In addition, the average age of congregational attenders is getting older. You might have heard that, because of the baby boomers, the average age of U.S. adults is increasing. However, in 2014, the average weekly attender was four years older than the average American adult, and this age difference has been growing over time. The declines in religiosity among younger generations are making it more challenging for congregations to recruit young adult attenders, and the aging of attenders is making it more difficult for some religious young adults to find a congregation where they feel like they belong. However, some congregations are finding opportunities and effective strategies for welcoming, embracing, and nurturing young adults in their faith.[3]

An additional challenge involves declining overall congregation sizes amid growing megachurches. This challenge is particularly impacting small and medium-sized congregations. According to recent research reported by the Religion News Service, "half of the country's congregations [have] 65 or fewer people in attendance on any given weekend, a drop from . . . 137 people in 2000."[4] Part of the decrease in size is related to the growth of megachurches. Over recent decades, in Protestantism, "people are becoming increasingly concentrated in the very largest churches, and this is true for small and large denominations, for conservative and liberal denominations, [and] for growing and declining denominations."[5] Although many large congregations have an explicit goal to recruit attenders who are "unchurched" or not already part of a local faith community, practically small and medium-sized congregations are shrinking largely because attenders are switching from smaller to larger congregations.[6]

Some congregations are in situations where their attenders do not match the people in their surrounding neighborhood in a variety of factors, including racial and ethnic backgrounds, education levels, incomes, and family types. In some situations, very few attenders live in or near the neighborhood in which their congregation is located. These changes can contribute to challenges in developing relationships with neighborhood residents, inviting residents to participate in religious services and congregational activities, and serving effectively in the surrounding neighborhood. Some congregations have turned these situations into opportunities to adapt and innovate their ministries for the community.[7]

The United States has recently experienced significant polarization related to politics and elections; views of gender and race; and responses to the pandemic, climate change, and other divisive issues, and congregations are not immune. In the midst of this polarization, frequent attendance at worship services is becoming more strongly associated with social and political conservatism. Some people who view the United States as an explicitly Christian nation may see this as an opportunity to "tak[e] America back for God," but others argue that Christian nationalism marginalizes people who do not fit a particular ideal, including people of color, immigrants, the LGBTQ+ community, religiously unaffiliated people, and people of a non-Christian faith. Most Americans aren't happy about this polarization, and a growing number of American adults oppose the influence of religion in politics. This polarization may create additional challenges for congregations to attract nonreligious people and young adults, who tend to be more politically progressive.[8] In addition, this polarization has created opportunities for some congregations to engage in intergroup dialogues and partnerships that build relationships, understanding, and collaborations across different faith traditions, racial and ethnic cultures, and gender and sexual identities.

There are also significant challenges facing congregational ministers and leaders. If you're a congregational minister or leader, it's not going to surprise you that many ministers and leaders invest a lot at their congregation, working well over forty hours a week. Juggling many responsibilities means that many ministers and leaders cannot spend as much time as they would like with family and friends and doing activities that they find restful and renewing. Despite the time, care, and love that many ministers and leaders seek to provide for their congregation, it's becoming harder because of changes in how Americans view religious leaders. It's particularly concerning to me that, since the 1970s, confidence in religious leaders has dropped sharply among not only U.S. adults generally but also people who regularly attend worship services. This drop is at least partly driven by clergy abuse scandals as well as concerns about religious leaders engaging in politics. All of these factors together create a difficult moment for doing ministry, and it's not surprising to me that many ministers and leaders are experiencing issues with physical health, mental health, and feelings of burnout, as well as that some ministers and leaders are seeking to leave ministry.[9]

As I've discussed these opportunities and challenges, you may have noticed that I have said very little in this section so far about the COVID-19 pandemic. This is because I want you to see how, before March 2020, congregations were already dealing with significant changes in their local communities and in American society that have created many opportunities and challenges for ministry. The pandemic, however, has brought about numerous changes, and congregations have differed in how prepared they have been to meet them. Based on guidance from public health experts, congregations largely switched to online and virtual worship and activities during the early months of the pandemic.[10] Some congregations already were streaming services and other events, but many congregations were not. This shift offered both challenges and opportunities for congregations to learn how to minister and/or to improve their ministry via virtual tools. Some congregations did not have the financial resources or technical infrastructure to stream their events, and numerous organizations, including Samford University's Center for Congregational Resources, have worked to equip congregations with these tools both before and during the pandemic.

During the course of the pandemic, many ministers and leaders had to make difficult decisions about the extent to which their congregation would be open for in-person events and the extent to which their congregation would

follow public health guidelines. About a quarter of congregations had significant conflict around how to respond to public health restrictions.[11] Here's how
a minister described this challenge.

> I don't know how to make this work. After a year of trying to assure people
> that we were still the church even when we weren't in the same room, I don't
> know how to convince them now of the importance of gathering in person. I
> know that if they are watching from home, fancier churches all over the country
> offer much slicker streamed services than our suburban church with its second-
> hand camera and duct-taped tripod. And no matter what we do, it isn't going to
> work for someone. A few families have started attending larger churches with
> more—or less—restrictive masking policies. I also know that kids' sports, held
> outdoors, have fewer restrictions, and that returning to a church habit after 20
> months away gets harder with each passing Sunday.[12]

These situations put many ministers and leaders between a rock and a
hard place.

With the shift to having at least some congregational events and services
offered virtually, some ministers and leaders have faced the new challenges
of understanding who is in their congregation and of maintaining relationships with attenders. Some congregations have expanded their reach and
attracted new attenders during the pandemic through their online events and
ministries. However, some of these new attenders have not yet shown up in
person, have not reached out to meet with a minister virtually, and do not even
live within driving distance. Other congregations have noticed that, although
there are some attenders who legitimately cannot worship in person for health
reasons and who are faithfully streaming online services, there are a number
of attenders who are not streaming or coming in person because their habits
have changed. Many ministers and congregational leaders are wondering if
these people will come back to services, contribute financially, or volunteer
at the congregation in the future.[13]

The pandemic also created opportunities for ministering in the community,
and many congregations have taken advantage of opportunities to provide
food, financial resources, and spiritual care to people in need in their congregations and communities. Some congregations became sites for COVID-19
testing and vaccinations. Congregations that, before the pandemic, already
had community-oriented ministries and partnerships with local community
organizations have been better equipped to respond to these opportunities.[14]

There have been concerns about ministers' physical and mental health
long before 2020, but things have been particularly difficult for many congregational ministers and leaders since the start of the pandemic. In a survey
conducted in 2021, two-thirds of the ministers shared that 2020 had been

their most challenging year in ministry, and things haven't necessarily gotten easier since. "After two years of a global pandemic, rabbis, pastors and other congregational leaders have given up predicting the future. Some say they are exhausted. Some are thinking about quitting. Others, while they are weary and the future is uncertain, say the pandemic has also brought opportunities for ministry and growth."[15] With the disruption caused by the pandemic, the necessity to innovate ministry, and the polarization around responses to the pandemic, many ministers and leaders have invested more time at their congregation, experienced more stress and conflict within their congregation, and received less support from their congregation—all of which contribute to burnout. As a result, a growing number of ministers and leaders are considering leaving or have left ministry.[16]

In the future, there will hopefully be less disruption to congregations' worship and activities, but many congregations will still experience serious ramifications from the COVID-19 pandemic. There are key long-term impacts around staffing and volunteers. Compared to pre-pandemic levels, many congregations have significantly fewer regular attenders who volunteer. In addition, numerous congregations eliminated paid staffing positions or reduced the hours they paid leaders to work. Through the pandemic, some congregations effectively adapted their ministries in the midst of the disruption, while other congregations struggled to navigate the changes, to sustain relationships with their attenders and communities, and to generate financial resources.[17] Many of these latter congregations will continue to experience difficulties, even as things get closer to normal in many contexts.

HOW RELATIONSHIPS PROVIDE SUPPORT

When we're going through difficult times, we can find support through relationships with others, and there are three key kinds of support that have helped congregations and their ministers and leaders to navigate opportunities and challenges. They're technically called emotional support, informational support, and instrumental support,[18] and each chapter will explore how these types of support are available (or not) in a particular relationship type.

Emotional support is the most common type of support, and it involves love, care, and a listening ear. It sounds something like this: "I care about you. I am here for you. I am sorry that this difficulty is happening, and I will stick with you through it." Many ministers share and value this type of support, and here's what two ministers have said about it. The first quote comes from a Presbyterian youth minister.

> Youth ministry needs networks to survive. We need encouragement. You work in a church setting and it's wonderful, but you're working for the church and sometimes you don't get as much encouragement as you'd like. So networking is very important for encouragement, edification, and also continuing education as I hang out with these other men and women.

The second quote comes from a pastor of a rural Southern Baptist church.

> I'm friends with most of [the nearby] pastors. I know just about all of them and usually talk to a majority of them during the week. It's just an encouragement to me, and I'm an encouragement to them, and we encourage one another congregation-wise too.

Emotional support can be very meaningful when congregations are navigating opportunities and challenges.

Informational support involves providing ideas, resources, and advice. Numerous ministers and leaders I've talked with have shared how important it has been to talk with other ministers and leaders, especially during the pandemic, about what has worked, what hasn't worked, and what's worth trying. A minister from a predominantly African American Baptist congregation described how relationships are

> meaningful in that I have a chance to look at what other people are doing. Sometimes it helps to gauge where you are, maybe where you need to be, and sometimes where you don't need to be. It's also good to have other ministers that can share problems and opportunities they've had and how they worked through them.

A nondenominational minister offered an example of how informational support has been valuable as he has received requests for COVID-19 vaccine exemptions, which his church does not want to provide. He's been able to brainstorm with other pastors who have received similar requests about how to respond. Many congregations benefit from sharing ideas and resources as they navigate various opportunities and challenges.

Instrumental support refers to practical, tangible assistance and, when shared among congregations, typically involves combining resources to collaborate. Here are three examples of collaborations that have helped congregations to expand their ministry in their communities. First, a middle school football coach asked a local Southern Baptist church to host the team for a meal and some time to hang out every week, and this church is now partnering with a number of nearby churches to serve this football team. Second, a rural church partners with local congregations to pool resources to provide food for children who get free school breakfasts and lunches but whose families may not be able to feed them during weekends. A third example involves a collaboration called Seek the Peace, which began among churches in a predominantly African American community; their goal is

> to get into the community to do more outreach and hold conversations with at-risk youth. That's the [primary] objective—not only to hold conversations with at-risk youth but to provide opportunities for at-risk youth and younger people that are of an age of employment, to get them employed, to provide scholarships and opportunities to get them in some form of training and education, and to provide some type of [after-school] activity, like sports.

Through sharing instrumental support, congregations can pool financial resources, leaders and volunteers, and space to minister in a way that they could not have done alone.

These types of support are valuable for congregations, their ministers, and their leaders, and congregations can develop supportive relationships in a variety of ways, including the following:

- friendships with ministers from other congregations
- joint events, including religious services, service projects, retreats, and conferences
- gatherings of ministers, including clergy peer groups and ministerial associations
- pulpit exchanges (preaching or teaching at another congregation or inviting another minister or leader to preach or teach at one's own congregation)[19]

Because many connections between congregations involve relationships between their ministers and leaders and because ministers' and leaders' well-being impacts congregational health, let's turn next to why relationships matter for ministers and leaders.

Why Relationships Matter for Ministers and Leaders

As I shared earlier, many ministers and leaders face challenges with stress, mental health, physical health, and burnout. Burnout can be described as "feeling strained as your emotional resources become depleted, becoming detached from, and cynical toward, the people you serve, and having doubts about how much you accomplish."[20] While there are many tools for helping people to recover from burnout, including exercise, sleep, and creative endeavors, a key tool involves social connection. Here's what one study found:

> A great strategy to maintain positive mental health is to foster strong friendships and relationships with partners, spouses, and family members. We found that pastors with flourishing mental health were more likely to have strong relationships than pastors with low mental health. Clergy are surrounded by people. However, we shouldn't confuse social interaction with supportive relationships. Clergy may interact with people all day, and they may frequently provide support to others, but that doesn't mean they're receiving support from others. . . . What are sources of emotional support for pastors? The most frequently mentioned sources were spouses, friends, and clergy colleagues.[21]

For congregational ministers and leaders, a variety of relationships are beneficial for health, and relationships with other ministers and leaders are particularly meaningful.[22]

For many ministers and leaders, it's important to have relationships with fellow ministers and leaders who understand what it's like to serve a congregation. One minister has shared that "my biggest thing is having someone to be accountable to. . . . I have a best friend. . . . We're both pastors, so we know the day-to-day stresses, and strains, and everything. We're able to relate [and] hold each other accountable."[23] These relationships are also important for ministers and leaders to guide congregations effectively, particularly in the midst of change and cultural disruption.

> In many conversations with pastors and denominational leaders . . . , the issue of clergy friendships emerged as of considerable importance for sustaining ministry in challenging times. Having close friends is in itself not a guarantee of excellent pastoral leadership; however, without the support, companionship, mutual critique, and joy that friends offer, without those with whom one can be vulnerable and share deeply, it is difficult, if not impossible, to sustain . . . [an] excellent ministry.[24]

Relationships between ministers and leaders can have positive impacts not only for ministers' and leaders' health and well-being but also within congregations. Congregations of ministers and leaders who regularly gather with others to learn and to support each other tend to have wider involvement in ministries and decision making among attenders, to integrate new attenders into the life of the congregation more effectively, and to be more engaged in ministry to their communities. There are additional ways in which relationships make a difference in congregations, and let's turn to this topic next.[25]

Why Relationships Matter for Congregations

Because the structure of the book, which I present in the next section, describes in more detail how different types of relationships impact congregations, I will keep this section fairly brief. As I share ministers' and leaders' stories in this book, we'll explore together how relationships between congregations can build trust and a shared purpose. Trust is an important foundation that allows congregations to provide support to each other in a variety of ways. Relationships with other congregations can provide a supportive setting for sharing about opportunities and challenges. Trust can make it easier for congregations to brainstorm, to strategize, and to share ideas and resources with other congregations about how to minister in the midst of change. Congregations can also develop collaborations through combining their resources to minister in ways that they could not have done alone.

TYPES OF RELATIONSHIPS AND THEIR IMPACT (AND WHAT TO EXPECT FOR THE REST OF THE BOOK)

As we explore how relationships help congregations to navigate opportunities and challenges, this book focuses on five different relationship types, each of which provides support for congregations, has pros and cons, and is the focus of a chapter. I provide practical tips for building different types of relationships near the end of most of the chapters and questions for your congregation to consider at the end of every chapter.

Chapter 2, "Birds of a Feather," focuses on relationships between congregations from the same religious group. Congregations are more likely to flock together with other congregations that belong to the same religious group, though many congregations have at least some relationships outside of their religious group. I define religious groups through Protestant denominations, nondenominational identities, and religious traditions for congregations outside of Protestantism (Roman Catholicism, Judaism, Islam, Eastern Orthodoxy, etc.). Relationships within religious groups (and between nondenominational churches) are very common due to their convenience. Many ministers and leaders feel like they have too much to do and not enough time to do it. While they may want to build relationships with other ministers, leaders, and congregations, they may not have much time to commit to doing so. Denominational (and nondenominational network) gatherings provide a convenient way for ministers and leaders to build relationships. In addition, relationships tend to be stronger and more trusting when a similarity is shared, and this trust can make it easier to share ideas and resources, to try new approaches, and to collaborate. There are two disadvantages for relationships within religious groups. First, these relationships can limit the range of ideas and resources available to congregations, and they can, in some cases, contribute to competition between congregations seeking to attract the same pool of attenders.[26]

Chapter 3, "Ties That Bind," focuses on a special subtype of relationships within religious groups—one where relationships within a particular religious group are so tight-knit that there are very few relationships between that religious group and other religious groups. This relationship type is most common among very distinctive religious groups, and two religious groups in this study stand out for having very tight-knit relationships almost exclusively within their religious group: nondenominational, noninstrumental Church of Christ congregations, which use no musical instruments in worship, and Church of Jesus Christ of Latter-day Saints wards. Tight-knit relationships can create supportive, trusting, and cooperative settings that may make it easier for congregations to open up about their opportunities and challenges and to seek advice and help from other trusted congregations. However, congregations with many tight-knit relationships often do not have access to a wider range of ideas and resources, and they may experience peer pressure that makes it harder to adapt and innovate.[27]

Chapter 4, "Bridging Near and Far," examines relationships between congregations from different religious groups. Theologically conservative congregations typically partner with congregations from other theologically conservative religious groups ("bridging near"), while theologically liberal churches and some non-Christian congregations tend to partner around social justice initiatives despite often significant theological differences between the religious groups ("bridging far"). Although this relationship type is not as common as relationships within religious groups, relationships between religious groups have many benefits for congregations. Relationships with congregations that have a different religious group can provide congregations with a wider range of information, ideas, resources, and opportunities for collaboration that can help them to respond to opportunities and challenges. Downsides include that these relationships can require more intentionality, that they are less convenient to develop, and that they do not tend to be as strong and close as relationships within religious groups.[28]

In my conversations with ministers and leaders, it was difficult to get them to talk much about relationships within racial groups, which is the topic of chapter 5, "Racial Barriers." Most congregations only or primarily interact with congregations that share the same racial composition; however, perhaps because of Alabama's legacies of racial injustice, ministers and leaders were hesitant to acknowledge a preference for relationships with other congregations with similar racial compositions. In this chapter, I focus on three barriers to relationships between congregations with different racial compositions. First, most religious groups in the United States draw ministers, leaders, and attenders primarily from one racial group, so congregations within a religious group are likely to share the same racial composition as well. Second, many congregations tend to build relationships with congregations in their local community. Because many communities in central Alabama are segregated by race, nearby congregations are likely to have the same racial composition. Third, many congregations in central Alabama are Evangelical and politically and theologically conservative. Because so many attenders at these churches supported former President Trump, who has inflamed racial tensions throughout the country, some ministers and leaders at predominantly African American congregations expressed concerns about developing relationships with predominantly white congregations due to differing views on racial inequality and justice.[29] Relationships within racial groups are typically easy and convenient to develop, but they reinforce racial segregations and divisions in central Alabama.

Chapter 6, "Partnering across Race," focuses on relationships between congregations with different racial compositions, which are not as common. These relationships are vitally important, particularly in central Alabama, because they help to counteract the racial inequality, segregation, and exclusion that still impact relationships between people of different races. However, these relationships can be more difficult to develop because ministers, leaders, and attenders from different racial groups often have different life experiences, approaches to faith, and cultural practices that need to be carefully considered in building a partnership. Some congregations have developed these relationships through racial reconciliation programs that match congregations of different racial compositions, and others have developed partnerships through building relationships more informally. Relationships between congregations from different racial groups have produced many fruitful collaborations because they can draw on a wider range of ideas and resources. Here are two examples I will share in this chapter: contractors and builders from predominantly white, suburban churches partnering with predominantly African American urban churches to address housing needs in low-income communities; predominantly white and predominantly African American congregations working together to oppose Confederate monuments in local parks.[30]

In chapter 7, "Practical Next Steps," I conclude the book by presenting practical next steps for congregations and their ministers and leaders. I start with four ways to build relationships with other congregations—joint events, friendships between ministers, gatherings of ministers, and pulpit exchanges. I also summarize insights from the book about the advantages and disadvantages of different relationships. My goal is to help you to identify the relationship types you're interested in developing and strengthening so that you can respond to the particular opportunities and challenges that your congregation is facing.

CENTRAL ALABAMA FOCUS WITH
BROADER PRACTICAL INSIGHTS

The stories and relationships I describe in this book are from central Alabama, so I'd like to introduce this context and how the book's insights are applicable in other contexts before we turn to chapter 2. The congregations I present in this book are from eight counties encompassing and surrounding the Birmingham-Hoover, Alabama, metropolitan statistical area. If you're interested, you can find a map of these counties in the appendix of this book.

Alabama is, in some ways, similar socially and religiously to other states in the southeastern United States but distinctive from many other U.S. states. It's predominantly politically conservative and Republican, and it's among the states that most strongly leaned toward former President Trump in the 2020 presidential election. Alabama is also among the states with the worst quality of education, health care, public health outcomes, and poverty rates. When it comes to religion, compared to other states, Alabama has one of the highest percentages of residents who are involved in a congregation (i.e., members, regular attenders, and children), the highest percentage of residents who are Evangelical Protestant, and one of the highest percentages of residents who are Southern Baptist. The five most common religious groups in the state (and in the eight-county study area) are the Southern Baptist Convention, the United Methodist Church, nondenominational congregations, the Catholic Church, and the National Baptist Convention, USA, Inc. (a historically African American denomination). You'll see these religious groups fairly frequently throughout this book.[31]

Within the eight counties that are the focus of this book, Birmingham is the largest city, and its origins lie in the steel industry. Geologically, a variety of minerals needed to produce steel—like iron ore, limestone, and coal—are available in the area. Birmingham also has a significant history related to racial oppression, segregation, and civil rights. It is among the ten most segregated cities in the United States, and it is also the home of Sixteenth Street Baptist Church, where a bombing killed four girls in 1963, the site of major civil rights events and protests; and the city from which Dr. Martin Luther King Jr. wrote his "Letter from a Birmingham Jail." Over time, Birmingham's economy has shifted more toward medicine, finance, and other industries, and it is the home of the University of Alabama at Birmingham (UAB) Hospital, the eighth largest hospital in the United States. In 2022, Birmingham hosted the World Games, an international event in which athletes from over thirty sports and over one hundred countries participated, and Birmingham is also increasingly known for its food, with numerous chefs winning national awards.[32] Tuscaloosa is the second largest city in this project's eight counties.

Tuscaloosa served as the Alabama state capital for part of the early nineteenth century, during which the University of Alabama was founded. In 1963, George Wallace, the Alabama governor, literally stood in a doorway to block African American students from enrolling at the university. Tuscaloosa was the site of a major natural disaster on April 27, 2011, when "a nearly mile wide tornado cut a path though the town, killing 53 people, and injuring 1200 more." The impact of this tornado is still visible in this community. Alabama Crimson Tide football with its famed coaches, like Bear Bryant and Nick Saban, is also a significant part of Tuscaloosa's culture.[33] In addition to Birmingham and Tuscaloosa, this book shares insights from congregations in a variety of suburban communities, small towns, and rural areas.

It's understandable if some of you are wondering whether this book has practical applications for your congregation in its context. Maybe you're from another geographic area that has different social, political, and religious characteristics. There are hundreds of religious groups across the United States, and perhaps your religious group isn't represented in this book. In Alabama, about 90 percent of people are non-Hispanic white or African American, and the congregations in this book are predominantly white, predominantly African American, or multiracial (typically with a combination of white, African American, and/or Hispanic attenders).[34] Your congregation may have a different racial composition.

This book's insights, however, are relevant within and beyond central Alabama because the two key social processes I focus on—social support and preferences for similarity—have been observed in a wide variety of situations. Social support takes place in friendships, marriages, work relationships, religious communities, medical settings, and many other social environments. It's such an important topic that there are over 100,000 scholarly studies that include "social support" in their title. There's lots of evidence that different kinds of support—including emotional, informational, and instrumental support—occur in numerous types of relationships with significant benefits. It's also common to prefer relationships with others who are similar to us in a wide variety of relationships, including friendships, marriages, organizational partnerships, and more. Chapters in this book focus on relationships within and between religious and racial groups because congregations are more likely to have relationships with religiously and racially similar congregations. This preference for similarity is so strong that some scholars have called it "one of our best established social facts" and "one of the most striking and robust empirical regularities of social life."[35] Because the types of support and the preferences to build relationships with others who are similar take place in so many different relationships and settings, the insights you'll find in this book are applicable for congregations in a wide variety of contexts.

A NOTE ABOUT STUDYING RELATIONSHIPS
BETWEEN CONGREGATIONS

Before we turn to chapter 2, I would also like to point you to the appendix if you would like more information about how I studied relationships between congregations in central Alabama. I am trying to keep the main text focused on stories from ministers and leaders and on practical insights for you, and I am putting the technical details in the appendix and in the notes at the end of the book. If you're interested in these details, please look there. Because significant changes occurred for congregations in early 2020 due to the pandemic, I will note here that I conducted the survey that I used to identify congregations' relationship types in 2017–2018, and that I conducted interviews with congregational ministers and leaders about how these relationship types impact how they respond to opportunities and challenges in the summer and fall of 2021.

Throughout the book, I show images that depict the relationships that are the focus of each chapter. I'd like to present the first image here so that you know what to expect. In my conversations with ministers, I learned about not just the *types* of relationships they have with other congregations but also *which* congregations they have relationships with. I have used this information to create a network of the relationships between congregations, which I present in figure 1.1. The appendix includes more detail about how I created the network.

Whenever I show these figures, people often ask what the clusters mean, so let's briefly focus on that before turning to chapter 2. I used a procedure that maximizes relationships within clusters and minimizes them between clusters to keep the image from looking too much like a bowl of spaghetti. (If you think it already looks like a bowl of spaghetti, that's fine, but the diagram would look much more convoluted without the clusters.) Sometimes people wonder if each cluster is a different religious group, but that's not the case. I am using the clusters just to provide structure within the network so that we can better see the relationship types as we proceed through the book.[36]

QUESTIONS TO CONSIDER

At the end of each chapter, I will offer some questions for your congregation to consider. These questions could be helpful to discuss with ministers, staff members, and other leaders. Here are some initial questions that subsequent chapters will build on.

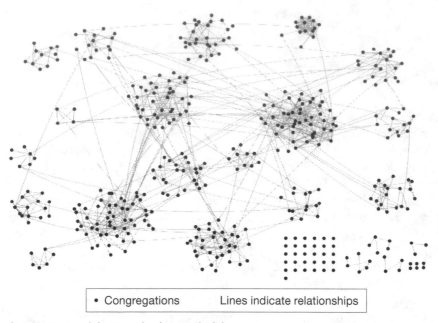

• Congregations   Lines indicate relationships

Figure 1.1.   Social Network of Central Alabama Congregations. Created by the author using NodeXL Basic (http://nodexl.codeplex.com) from the Social Media Research Foundation (https://www.smrfoundation.org).

1. With which congregations does your congregation have relationships?
2. What is the religious group of each congregation?
3. What is the racial composition of each congregation?
4. What opportunities and challenges is your congregation experiencing?

I encourage you to create a list of around ten congregations. I'm suggesting ten because it's manageable, but you're welcome to list more or fewer congregations. In your list, include each congregation's name, religious group, and racial composition.

Chapter 2

Birds of a Feather

When ministers and leaders want to build relationships with other congregations, it is often easiest to start within their religious group. Many congregational ministers and leaders are faced with the challenge of having too much to do and not enough time to do it. Sound familiar? Most ministers and leaders work well over forty hours a week preaching and teaching, leading and preparing for worship, providing care and counsel, administrating programs, attending meetings, and more. As a result, many ministers and leaders find it difficult to carve out enough time to spend with their family and friends, to engage in hobbies, and to rest. So if ministers and leaders feel like they have limited time to build relationships with other congregations and are offered some opportunities to do so, do you think they will choose a more convenient or less convenient option?[1]

Most congregations build relationships primarily within their religious group.[2] So that it's clear, here's how I'm defining a religious group. For Protestant churches that have a denominational affiliation, their religious group is their denomination. I am considering nondenominational Protestant churches as sharing the same religious group, with a few exceptions.[3] For congregations that are not Protestant, like Eastern Orthodox, Jewish, Muslim, and Roman Catholic congregations, I am defining their religious group as their religious tradition (Eastern Orthodoxy, Judaism, Islam, and Roman Catholicism), despite different movements and jurisdictions within some of these religious groups. Throughout this book, I use the term *religious group* instead of *denomination* because *denomination* is typically not used by non-Protestant religious groups to describe themselves.

Figure 2.1 shows how relationships between congregations are more common when the congregations share the same religious group. (Nondenominational churches are also more likely to have relationships with other nondenominational churches.) Fifty-seven percent of the relationships in this diagram (455 of 793) are between congregations that share the same religious group. This chapter focuses on why relationships within religious

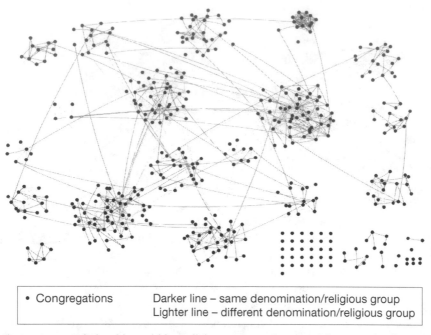

| • Congregations | Darker line – same denomination/religious group |
| | Lighter line – different denomination/religious group |

Figure 2.1. Relationships within Religious Groups in a Social Network of Central Alabama Congregations. Created by the author using NodeXL Basic (http://nodexl. codeplex.com) from the Social Media Research Foundation (https://www.smrfounda- tion.org).

groups are so convenient, the types of support they offer, how congregations use these relationships to navigate opportunities and challenges, and the drawbacks of these relationships.

CONVENIENCE MATTERS

Many religious groups have regional or local bodies in which their congre- gations participate, like a local Baptist association, a regional Presbyterian presbytery, a Methodist district, or a Catholic or Episcopal diocese. Although these bodies have different organizational and leadership structures, they all seek to provide their congregations, ministers, and leaders with opportunities to gather, to share resources, and to collaborate. For ministers and leaders who have too much to do and not enough time to do it, these gatherings are often the most convenient way to build relationships with other ministers, leaders, and congregations.[4]

In addition, growing numbers of nondenominational churches are build- ing relationships, exchanging ideas, and developing partnerships through nondenominational networks. A key point of connection for some nondenominational churches in Alabama is the Association of Related Churches (ARC). ARC is not a denomination but a network of leaders and churches that support church planting or starting new Christian congregations. The leadership team for ARC is made up of ministers from nondenominational congregations across the United States and includes ministers from a megachurch in Alabama. Churches around the world, whether or not they have a denominational affiliation, can participate in ARC by receiving support as a new church plant or by contributing financial and other resources to support new church plants.[5] Many nondenominational churches are also finding convenient settings for building relationships with similar congregations.

Here are four reasons why relationships within religious groups (or between nondenominational churches) are so convenient.

1. Especially with the disruption congregations have experienced because of COVID-19, these relationships are a lot easier. A minister at a Presbyterian Church (U.S.A.) congregation that has many relationships across religious groups shared, "If I'm honest, in the last year and a half, a lot of it has been in-house PC(USA) talk just because that was easier."

2. A preference for relationships within a religious group is common in many religious groups. A Christian Methodist Episcopal minister who has numerous relationships with congregations from different religious groups shared, "In our denomination, we are kind of locked in, I guess, to the thought of not really visiting or connecting with other denominations, other than maybe if somebody invites me to preach or work in the community, which is problematic for me. So I can see why [relationships within the denomination] would be easier."

3. Shared theological views and approaches to ministry make it easier to collaborate. For a rural Southern Baptist church, sharing the same religious group "would make partnering with other churches easier. It would not be difficult at all to plan a joint revival because people are going to have the same ideas of what that means and what you want to accomplish. So for the most part, that would be easy."

4. There is a shared organizational structure for collaborations. A nondenominational minister described how "it's so much easier to work with nondenominational churches because [a friend who is a minister at a Baptist church] can't give me an answer until he talks to this board or that board, and every single thing [nondenominational churches] do does not have to be voted on or discussed by another group of people."

BENEFITS OF RELATIONSHIPS
WITHIN RELIGIOUS GROUPS

There are three key types of support that congregations can offer to each other, and sharing the same religious group makes it easier for congregations to provide and receive these types of support.

Trusting, Encouraging Friendships

When we go through difficult times, emotional support matters. Having someone in our lives who can say something like, "I'm sorry you're going through this. I am here for you, I care about you, and I support you," can make a huge difference. It's easier for ministers and leaders to develop trusting, encouraging relationships within their religious group because having a shared approach to theology and ministry strengthens trust.[6] A pastor at an Independent Fundamentalist church expressed how theological agreement is related to trust: "It starts with being on the same page doctrinally. We would trust that nobody would be trying to teach error or lead people astray or anything like that. If we were working together on a project, we'd have confidence that things were done right. So doctrinal-likeness and like-mindedness is where I think our unity would start." This trust helps ministers to encourage each other and to be more honest about struggles within religious groups. Here are three more examples. A pastor at a rural Southern Baptist church said that "pastors in our county get together once a month. A lot of churches are taking a big hit, just with people leaving. To be able to get together and encourage one another just to keep pressing on and doing what the Lord has called us to do, that helps because a lot of pastors out there don't have that kind of encouragement." The second example comes from a minister at a nondenominational ARC church who explained how "it's just good to be able to say, 'Hey, this is what I'm doing. What are you doing?' And then, on a personal level, it's just good to say, 'What the heck man, I want to quit. Me too. Let's go have lunch.'" A minister at a Southern Baptist church outside of Tuscaloosa provided the third example: "I love being able to call and just be like, 'Hey, can I pick your brain a quick second?' They're willing to chat with me." It's often easier within religious groups for ministers and leaders to reach out for and to provide emotional support.

Exchanging Ideas and Resources

When we're going through a difficult time, we sometimes need more than just emotional support. We might need information, ideas, and resources to help us to navigate the challenging situations we find ourselves in. Religious groups provide congregations with resources and also with opportunities to exchange ideas and resources, and congregations are often more likely to trust these ideas and resources because of the shared religious identity.[7] A Southern Baptist pastor shared an example of how its local Baptist association has provided helpful resources: "I'm not a counselor. I will listen, but after one or two sessions, we're going to find a professional Christian counselor, and we usually do that through our Baptist association." A minister at a suburban Presbyterian Church in America congregation also regularly exchanges ideas and resources at presbytery meetings. "So I go there looking for resources, and I go there offering my resources to help them anyway I can. I just feel like the network that we have, there's high confidence in what I'm doing and what I can share with other churches because of the relationships."

These ideas and resources have become even more important in recent years. In the midst of significant disruption from the COVID-19 pandemic, many religious groups provided convenient ways for congregations to strategize together. A minister at a nondenominational ARC church has been grateful for opportunities to ask "questions like, 'What are you doing that I should be doing? What's working for you?' or even, 'What have you done that has not worked, so that I know to stay away from things like that?'" A Southern Baptist minister also described the importance of brainstorming and sharing ideas with other Southern Baptist ministers.

> We've been sharing ideas of, when we go back [to in-person worship], what we're going to do that will really make sense with our congregations—how we can have a more hands free worship, not taking offering, how we are going to handle Communion, and how we're going to do the bulletin. We came up with this idea that we're going to email the bulletin, so if a person wants a bulletin, then they can go to their email. Since about 60 percent of the congregation bought into online giving, we'll continue that and make ways that, at the beginning of worship, others can drop off the [financial] gift. If it's Communion Sunday, they can pick up Communion when they come in. So we've been exchanging ideas.

It's often easiest for congregations to find ideas and resources within their religious group, and they are more likely to use this information because of the trusting relationships within the religious group.

Collaborations

Have you ever tried to do something difficult and felt like you needed something in addition to emotional support and information? Sometimes we need people to come alongside us and to collaborate with us to do what we need to do. When organizations share a similarity, collaborations tend to be more convenient to develop,[8] and this is certainly true for congregations that share the same religious group. A Presbyterian Church in America minister shared how theological similarity makes collaborations easier: "Because we do come into a shared belief about what it is that we believe the Bible teaches, that helps us to actually do things together without always fighting over whether we agree. If we didn't agree, then it would be difficult for us to do anything together because we would be constantly arguing." A rural Southern Baptist minister provided another example of how it has been easier to develop evangelistic partnerships with fellow Southern Baptist churches.

> We help a lot of churches with evangelism [or proselytization] and discipleship [or helping people "to follow Jesus Christ"[9]] because a lot of churches don't do door-to-door evangelism anymore. We would not limit our visitation to just Baptist churches. We would help churches in need, but the Baptist churches have been most open for us to come in to do [evangelistic] work.

The trust developed within religious groups makes it easier to develop collaborations.

For some congregations, collaborations within their religious group are particularly meaningful because other congregations are hesitant to partner with them because of theological differences or misunderstandings. A Seventh-day Adventist minister shared that "people don't really know who we are. They think we're a mix of Mormons and Jehovah's Witnesses, so they're wary of us." Because of this, it's been easier for this church to collaborate with other Adventist churches to do evangelism and to address community issues.

These collaborations help congregations to do more than they can do alone. A suburban Southern Baptist minister shared that being part of the Birmingham Metro Baptist Association "gives us opportunities to do things that we cannot do on our own, where we're able to reach and help and be a part of a larger, more influential group because we're all together." Similarly, a rural Southern Baptist pastor values

> really leveraging that relationship [with the local Baptist association] to understand what events are going on at different churches and how we can help in other areas because our goal is to expose people to Christ. So whether it's through something at [our church] or something through another church, we want to make sure that we can maximize that effort in every way that we can.

In addition, a regional leader in the Christian Methodist Episcopal Church shared how, during the pandemic, CME churches were able to provide Meals on Wheels and food through the Farmers to Families initiative that the federal government launched. Through working with churches from [across Alabama], we sent 18-wheelers and distributed over 750,000 pounds of produce, meats, vegetables, milk, and cheeses, and we were just so delighted to be able to do that over a four-month period during COVID. While we provided that food, we also provided COVID testing, and now I'm working with another organization to bring COVID vaccinations into rural areas as well.

Collaborations within religious groups often provide the most convenient ways for congregations to pool resources and expand the impact of their ministry.

NAVIGATING OPPORTUNITIES AND CHALLENGES TOGETHER WITHIN RELIGIOUS GROUPS

In this section, I'd like to give you some examples of how congregations are using relationships within their religious group to navigate specific opportunities and challenges. Because relationships within religious groups are so common, I'm probably giving too many examples here, but hopefully some of them resonate for you.

A Suburban Southern Baptist Church

This church values evangelism and missions. Its minister shared that "we are ourselves on reaching out to our local community and to our larger community through sharing the Gospel, showing the love of Christ. We've been involved in ministries and missions, trying to reveal the grace that comes from salvation through Jesus." Its goal is for its ministries to be "very Christ centered" and "very scripturally focused."

However, the pandemic has disrupted some of its evangelistic efforts. Relationships with other Southern Baptist congregations through a local Baptist association have helped with navigating this challenge. According to this church's minister,

Birmingham Metro [Baptist Association] is a strong relational network as well as a strong missional network. We're all seeking ways to influence our communities. We're all facing the challenge of keeping God's word faithfully in the midst of a shifting culture. You get in a group of pastors, and you find that most of us are dealing with the same sorts of opportunities reaching new people, providing new ministries, and trying to be proactive in what we are doing in ministries and missions.

Collaborations are built into the fabric of the Southern Baptist Convention, where churches are encouraged to "cooperate with one another in carrying forward the missionary, educational, and benevolent ministries for the extension of Christ's Kingdom."[10] This church has previously collaborated with other local SBC churches to do evangelistic work, including during the SBC annual meeting held in Birmingham in 2019, and this church is collaborating with Southern Baptist partners to plan its post-pandemic evangelistic work. This minister described how "we have a mission opportunity headed to Toronto, there are some opportunities in central America that we're looking toward, as well as being very actively involved with the mission outreach of the Southern Baptist Convention through our involvement and financial support. That's a very important part of who we are." This church has navigated disruptions to its evangelistic work and prepared for future evangelistic opportunities through its Southern Baptist relationships.

A Nondenominational Multisite Church

This congregation does not have a denominational affiliation and has multiple worship locations across different communities. It is also part of the Association of Related Churches (ARC), the nondenominational church planting network I mentioned earlier in this chapter. This church's mission is to strengthen individuals, families, and communities by helping people to know God, to be transformed in how they live, and to serve and make a difference.

Relationships within ARC have helped this church to navigate opportunities and challenges related to attendance, changes in worship, and outreach during the COVID-19 pandemic. One of its ministers shared, "Our attendance has been all over the place during the entire thing." Service formats also changed throughout the pandemic from "online services; then meeting in small house churches; and, today, just large service gatherings. So that's definitely been a challenge coaching and leading people through that with all sorts of opinions." The pandemic also provided opportunities for outreach and community service. In outreach toward people who are not part of a local church, this minister shared that "with the coronavirus, what we've started to see is that people are looking for a new normal, and so people that maybe weren't open to church before coronavirus, now they're open to church." Relationships within ARC have provided friendship, resources, and support. This minister is thankful for how "the pastors in this network are great about encouraging one another, being there for one another. We're able to gather ideas and ministry techniques [related to] responding to COVID and outreach." For outreach, this minister described how there's a big emphasis from ARC that we don't want to have pockets of our cities that we're not reaching, so some of those missing pieces guide us to where our outreach should be, and not just in terms of racial or economic diversity but really even just as simple as using zip codes. If we're not seeing any visitor cards from [a particular] zip code, we need to get there with a Serve project.

ARC supports this church's community outreach with an app that helps churches to communicate with their attenders about opportunities to serve in the community, to coordinate volunteers during the service event, and to collect stories and facilitate social media engagement during and after the event.[11]

An Episcopal Parish in Birmingham

Through its worship and ministries in the community, this Episcopal parish seeks "to share the Good News and to serve our neighbors." There are strong relationships within this parish. Its priest described how, before the pandemic, "when we shared The Peace [a liturgical greeting that conveys God's love and acceptance[12]] after the announcements and before the Communion Liturgy, everybody would get out of their pews, hug each other, pat each other on the back, talk to each other. It's a very welcoming, interactive parish."

It's also a relatively small parish, and the pandemic has negatively impacted attendance. Due to having fewer attenders, this church has limited financial resources for building maintenance and other ministry endeavors. This congregation's main ministry toward the community is a food pantry, to which other Episcopal parishes have contributed financial support and volunteers. According to the priest, relationships with other Episcopal parishes "are the kind of connections that if I'm in a terrible need, I can pick up the phone, and I know people in so many different towns in Alabama that I could ask for help, and they'd be there in a heartbeat." This parish has also expanded its opportunities for ministry through partnerships within its diocese. Here's a recent example. The priest shared how, in collaboration with other Episcopal parishes, "we're having a program that is open to anyone across the diocese, or they don't have to be Episcopal. It's called Conversations Across Difference." The goal is "just to bring people together during this time of social unrest and not try to fix everything but just to build relationships because there are all kinds of differences. It doesn't have to be racial. It can be age or stage of life or whatever." Collaborations within the Episcopal diocese are providing this parish with ministry opportunities that it might not be able to undertake on its own.

A United Methodist Church in Tuscaloosa

This church's mission is to grow spiritually, to show love to others, and to engage in the community. Its pastor described how it is "very involved in mission efforts around the community and the world. We support foreign missionaries, but we give a tremendous amount of support to local agencies. We've worked through partnerships and a lot of hands-on stuff as well." This church has "an openness to seekers, to doubters, to people who are not convinced of [the faith's] story yet; they pride themselves on being a safe place for those conversations. They are focused theologically in terms of the Great Commandment—love God and love others—and the rest works itself out when you do those."

Key challenges include navigating the pandemic and denominational conflict over sexuality. The pandemic has changed the ways in which this church worships and serves in its community. The pastor shared, "We have honored CDC guidelines and protocols, which has meant we've had to learn how to worship online. Everything we do now is live streaming. We do have a significantly smaller crowd in worship than we used to have but with social distancing and masking." Before the pandemic, this church had a partnership with a local school to provide tutors but has since shifted to providing books for children at the school. In addition, this church is also discerning next steps amidst the continued conflict within the broader United Methodist Church about sexuality. Relationships within the United Methodist Church have been helpful for support and sharing ideas. Its minister shared,

> My relationships with other clergy have been certainly helpful in mutual support, mutual prayer, and guidance from one another. We've leaned on one another for advice and counsel as we've tried to navigate the pandemic and especially about how to navigate the denominational issues. We've met quite a few times to try to imagine what's coming and figure out how to get through it.

Relationships within a religious group are often quite trusting and supportive. This example shows how these relationships can be particularly meaningful when there is significant difficulty facing a specific religious group, like a denomination-wide conflict.

A Southern Baptist Church West of Birmingham

This church has a strong emphasis on discipleship and outreach to the community. One of its ministers described how its mission involves "making disciples and those disciples making other disciples. [They] do a lot of community outreach events and try to be an anchor in [their] community." This church offers a variety of events and seeks to connect with people who "don't have any connections with any churches, or if they do, it's very marginal."

Ministers at this church are concerned about Christian nominalism, both within the church and in its community, and see discipleship and outreach as tools to address it. According to this minister, "Being in a culture that is very familiar with the Gospel and with Jesus Christ, at least on a surface level, has created an environment where a lot of churchgoers will come on Sunday morning. They do it really just because it's something they've always done, and there's not a real understanding of what following Christ really means or entails." This church has drawn on relationships with other Southern Baptist churches to strengthen its opportunities for discipleship and outreach. Before the pandemic, this church's minister was gathering with other local Southern Baptist ministers monthly. "What was significant about it is, it helped us feel like we're not in competition with each other. We're all working for the same thing. We prayed together and challenged each other." These relationships have led to ministers preaching at each other's churches as well as collaborations for addiction recovery ministries, Upward Basketball, youth events, and mission trips. Resources can flow very easily between these Southern Baptist churches. This minister shared, "Several years ago, we did a fall festival, and there were no churches in our area doing one. The next year, one of the churches close by said they were going to try it at their church, and we shared with them how we gathered people's contact information and then reached out to them afterwards. Now we didn't do a fall festival this year because everybody else is doing one." According to this minister, the shared denominational background makes it easier to build these relationships and partnerships. "We're all cut from the same cloth, so it's easy to team up with each other and to exchange ideas. There is definitely not a lot of crossing denominational lines as far as partnerships go. It's not that we're against that, but we've never really been intentional about doing it. In our immediate area, there are not really any other denominations."

A Catholic Parish in Birmingham

This predominantly African American Roman Catholic parish has had a significant history during civil rights in Birmingham, and this period still plays an important role in the parish's identity. However, the neighborhood has shifted over recent decades. This parish's priest described how "it's becoming a little more gentrified. The racial character of the neighborhood is not 100 percent Black anymore. There are white couples and Hispanic couples and families moving in because it's a beautiful neighborhood and people are taking advantage of it."

This parish experiences challenges with some poverty and safety issues in its neighborhood and with generating financial resources for its ministries, and there are opportunities to expand its ministry toward children and families in its neighborhood. The priest at this parish described how relationships tend to be more common among local Catholic parishes because of their shared approach to theology and worship. Relationships with clergy at other parishes have been an important source of support for this parish's priest. "If we are friends and we get along, then the cooperation between the parishes is very effective and very good. They're cooperative, and they're supportive. Because [my parish is] so small, if I get into some trouble, they're willing to help me, and they have helped me." The Catholic diocese has also provided resources and opportunities for collaboration for this parish. The priest explained that

> if it's taken advantage of, it's a great asset. There are six programs [run by the diocese] that directly affect my parish on a regular basis, from catechesis, to religious formation, to liturgy, to music, and also help for the poor. A lot of our resources will go directly to them because they do a better job of helping the poor than we would on an individual basis, especially using facilities such as the Catholic Center of Concern. They served twenty-one thousand people last year, and part of our money goes to them.

Partnerships within the Catholic Church have helped this parish to find resources for its ministries and have strengthened its impact in the community.

A Predominantly African American Baptist Church in Birmingham

This National Baptist church values being a multigenerational church with attenders from great-grandparents through children. Its desire to minister across generations shapes its approach to worship, which includes both hymns and contemporary Gospel music. Its pastor shared how "there's only one audience in worship, and that's God. We are here to entertain Him, not to entertain us. We have [a wide range of worship styles] so that all ages can relate to what's going on."

The pandemic has impacted this church and its outreach to the community in particular. The pastor explained, "We have had for several years a very active feeding program here, where we gave food to our elderly and our handicapped. COVID-19 has closed our kitchen. We still try to reach out by supporting ministries that are out there, like United Way," some foreign missionary organizations, and partner churches in other countries. The pastor at this church has held leadership positions in a local Baptist association, and relationships within this group have been helpful for sharing resources about how to worship during the pandemic and for collaborating to minister in the community. The pastor described the following:

> I am trying to teach pastors how to make better use of the ministry tools that we have. A lot of older ministers, it's hard for them to preach online, to preach in an empty building, because a lot of our preaching in the Afro American community is call and response. They've been so used to call and response that it's difficult for them to preach in an empty room, so we're trying our best to get them to understand that we're still reaching people.

Because much of this church's ministry in its community has been limited by the pandemic, here's an example of a community collaboration pre-2020. This collaboration reflects this church's commitment to minister to every generation. The pastor shared,

> Before COVID-19, we had a summer camp here at the church. I got the idea from another church in our cluster who had a successful summer camp, and I got assistance from them. One of the churches in my cluster that had a feeding program supplied the food. We took the children on field trips, and sometimes we had to use transportation from other churches because we didn't have enough vehicles to take all of the kids.

The close relationships within this local Baptist association have allowed this church's pastor to help other ministers to navigate preaching during the pandemic and have helped this church to expand its opportunities to serve in its community.

A Rural Cowboy Church

This church is affiliated with the American Fellowship of Cowboy Churches.[13] According to its pastor, this church seeks to reach people in rural communities who "don't go to church, don't—for some reason—feel accepted in church, don't feel comfortable, don't want to go to church. Those are the people we go after." This church worships both inside and outside of its building, hosts rodeos, and leads trail rides. Since the pandemic started, this church has experienced changes in how it worships and in participation. The pastor described how "since COVID, we've had to go to Facebook Live for our services." In ministering to people who are already not attracted to traditional churches, "our challenge is also that a lot of people do not feel comfortable coming to church anymore because of COVID." This church's orientation toward the outdoors has helped it to navigate changes in worship during the pandemic. "We have chuck wagon breakfasts now once a month, and so we're out doing that instead of in the church itself. Our people are more outdoor people than some churches are and feel more comfortable doing it that way."

Relationships with other nearby Cowboy churches have supported this church in reaching out to rural communities, in collaborating for ministry opportunities, and in navigating changes during the pandemic. Many Cowboy pastors in Alabama helped to start the first Cowboy church east of the Mississippi River. The pastor shared, "We separated to go out and witness to the people in our locations. So we started churches in these little communities. They're not big, because we're looking for a certain type of person, and it doesn't fit everybody. We are trying to just minister to the people that don't have a church or don't feel comfortable in a church." There are many friendships among these Cowboy churches, and these relationships are strengthened by joint worship services and activities. When this particular church is hosting a joint worship service, the pastor described what would happen: "I don't do the service. My worship team doesn't do the service. We have a different music team and a different pastor come in. A lot of people will come because we're all friends and want to see each other and worship together." This pastor shares how Cowboy churches have collaborated through their denomination to offer "a camp for teens and pre-teens. All of their churches in Alabama and Tennessee, their kids go to this camp, and so they grow up knowing each other," and these relationships are then reinforced after camp when teens go to rodeos at each other's churches. Relationships with other Cowboy pastors have also been helpful for discerning how to worship during the pandemic. The pastor explained, "I've met with other pastors, and I've seen what other pastors are doing. Different times, we've closed churches. Some churches have gone and done different ways of meeting. We might mimic them or take some of their ideas and try them so that our people are able to come and feel comfortable." This Cowboy church's unique mission and culture have led to strong relationships and collaborations with other Cowboy churches.

DOWNSIDES OF RELATIONSHIPS
WITHIN RELIGIOUS GROUPS

While it's very convenient to develop relationships within a religious group, these relationships do have some drawbacks. One involves the range of ideas and resources that congregations can learn about within their religious group. A minister at a nondenominational ARC church described how

> the advantage is you're all doing similar things and you can really pick up some cool stuff, and the disadvantage is that you're all doing similar things, and you can have that kind of groupthink. I don't want to just think about what ARC

churches are saying. I want to think about my mother's [denominational] church and want to think about the [Eastern] Orthodox priest I had dinner with not so long ago and what they bring.

Another disadvantage is that there can be competition between congregations within the same religious group for attenders. A minister at a predominantly African American Baptist church shared that "I get more support from churches that are not in this area than churches that are. I preach all over, but local is almost hard to break that mold because some are afraid that people will leave a church and come and join [my church]." A rural Southern Baptist minister experienced similar challenges.

> If you're in a Southern Baptist church in Blount County, it's going to look pretty much like the other ones. One of the downfalls or negatives of that homogeneity is that there is a certain—I'm not sure competition is the right word—but you're trying to reach the same people. That makes it a bigger deal when somebody leaves your church and goes to a different church. That hinders really working together.

Sharing a religious group can limit the range of information available to congregations and can hinder cooperation in situations where congregations are trying to attract the same attenders.

TIPS FOR YOUR CONGREGATION

If you're a minister or leader affiliated with a religious group or denomination and you're looking to build more relationships within your religious group, here are some practical tips.

- Go to religious group or denominational events! Many things can go on at these events, including conversations about policies, initiatives, conflicts, and other things. Hopefully, though, your gatherings are not all about Robert's Rules of Order and decision making. One of the most important things that these events can and should nurture is relationships between ministers and leaders.
- Be intentional about building connections that you can engage in outside of these events. Build friendships with ministers and leaders with whom you can go and get coffee or a meal. Try to invest the time it takes to build trust and a closer relationship.
- Reach out to each other when you need support. Sometimes in ministry, especially when we are focused on pouring into and investing in our

congregations, it can be hard to admit when we need help and support. Closer and more trusting relationships typically provide more emotional support, encourage more frequent sharing of ideas and resources, and can lead to the most in-depth collaborations.

If you're a nondenominational minister or leader and you'd like to build more relationships with nondenominational churches, you can find opportunities to do so, but it might take more intentionality.

- Reach out to nondenominational ministers and leaders in your community. Get to know each other over coffee or a meal, and spend time getting to know each other's churches. Set aside time to pray, learn about common interests, and support each other.
- Look into nondenominational networks. There are a growing number of options around the United States, and they can have different theological orientations and ministry focuses. Perhaps other nondenominational ministers and leaders can suggest options. Finding a network that fits your church's identity may provide more opportunities to gather with and learn from other congregations.

RECAP AND WHAT'S NEXT

Religious groups and nondenominational networks provide convenient ways for ministers and leaders to get to know each other and to build connections between their congregations. Because congregations within the same religious group tend to flock together, relationships within religious groups provide convenient ways for congregations to build trust, to share ideas and resources, and to collaborate. However, relationships within religious groups may limit the ideas and resources that congregations can learn about, and they can, in some situations, contribute to competition with similar congregations for attenders.

In chapter 3, we explore a subtype of relationships within religious groups, which involves relationships that are almost exclusively within a particular religious group. Congregations that draw most or all of their relationships from within their religious group are typically not isolated from other religious groups, because they or other congregations within their religious group have at least some relationships with congregations from other religious groups. However, some distinctive religious groups are so tight-knit that it's rare for their congregations to have relationships outside of their religious group, and this chapter focuses on examples from noninstrumental Church of Christ congregations and Church of Jesus Christ of Latter-day Saints wards. These tight-knit relationships can create very supportive, trusting, and cooperative settings, but they can limit access to a wider range of ideas and resources and constrain the extent to which congregations can adapt when responding to opportunities and challenges.

QUESTIONS TO CONSIDER

1. How many of the congregations on your list are in your religious group?
2. How did you develop these relationships?
3. What support have you offered or received through them?
4. How can you use insights from this chapter to create and strengthen relationships within your religious group?
5. How might these relationships help your congregation to navigate its opportunities and challenges and to support other congregations?

Chapter 3

Ties That Bind

Although congregations in many religious groups have a preference for relationships within their religious group, some religious groups stand out because congregations have relationships almost exclusively within their religious group, with very few relationships outside of their religious group. You might have been part of or been aware of social groups like this throughout your life. I remember calling them *cliques* in middle and high school. These groups can provide very rich support, but they can isolate members and create significant peer pressure to conform to the group's ideals. This is true not only for people as individuals but also for congregations as organizations.

This chapter focuses on relationships within two distinctive religious groups: (1) the nondenominational, noninstrumental Churches of Christ and (2) the Church of Jesus Christ of Latter-day Saints. Latter-day Saints leaders and members are more frequently calling their church the "Church of Jesus Christ," but I will be referring to it either with its full name or as "Latter-day Saints" so that it is clear which group I am talking about as we proceed through the chapter. My research on central Alabama congregations has found that, for both religious groups, all but one of their congregations draw all of their relationships from within their own religious group, and you might notice how the tight-knit relationships among Church of Christ and Latter-day Saints congregations stand out in figure 3.1.

This chapter explores why relationships are so tight-knit within the Churches of Christ and within the Church of Jesus Christ of Latter-day Saints, the support that these tight-knit relationships offer within these religious groups, and the downsides of these relationships. It differs from the previous chapter in two ways. Because I do not have as many interviews to draw on for this chapter (due to its focus on smaller religious groups) and because congregations within these religious groups know each other so well, I am not including as much information about how congregations are using these relationships to navigate *specific* opportunities and challenges. In addition, I do not offer practical tips for how to develop these relationships. My advice

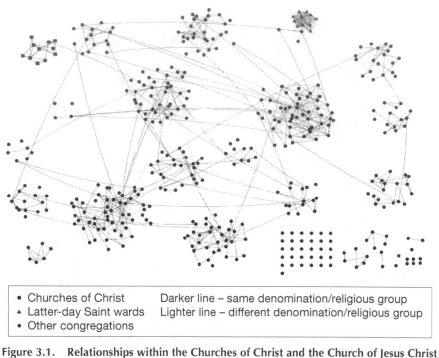

- ■ Churches of Christ   Darker line – same denomination/religious group
- ▲ Latter-day Saint wards   Lighter line – different denomination/religious group
- • Other congregations

Figure 3.1.   Relationships within the Churches of Christ and the Church of Jesus Christ of Latter-day Saints in a Social Network of Central Alabama Congregations. Created by the author using NodeXL Basic (http://nodexl.codeplex.com) from the Social Media Research Foundation (https://www.smrfoundation.org).

would not differ from what I shared in chapter 2, and these relationships are specific to certain religious groups and are not available to most ministers and congregations.

WHY THE CHURCHES OF CHRIST AND
THE LATTER-DAY SAINTS?

Some of you reading this book might be familiar with these two religious groups, but I'm not going to assume that all of you are. Let's start with introductions to each of these groups and then turn to why relationships are so tight-knit within these religious groups.

The Churches of Christ are part of the Restoration movement. This movement began in the early 1800s and is oriented "around the notion of restoration—the striving to return to New Testament Christianity."[1] A concern that motivated two of this movement's founders, Alexander and Thomas Campbell, was the division among Christian denominations and groups, and the Campbells "felt that a restoration of the New Testament would include a union of all Christians."[2] Restoration leaders sought to unite Christians around biblical teachings without an overarching denomination.

> They protested the division of Christianity, which they called a result of sectarian ideas (as expressed in creeds) and church polity not based on the Bible. They took "Bible only" as their uniting creed. . . . They did not like any structures that either usurped the duties of the local church (as mission societies did) or that exerted power over the church, as some Baptist associations, presbyteries, or bishops did.[3]

This movement has, over time, divided into different denominations and nondenominational groups. The Churches of Christ are the most prominent Restoration group in Alabama. They are nondenominational and autonomous, with no organization governing or overseeing them, and they are bound together by a shared, conservative understanding of the Bible: "Where the Scriptures speak, we speak; where the Scriptures are silent, we are silent."[4] Despite their autonomy, there is widespread agreement in belief and practice among Churches of Christ. They typically do not use instruments in worship, and many Churches of Christ view noninstrumental worship as an essential part of their identity.[5]

The Latter-day Saints movement was founded by Joseph Smith in the early 1800s. He also was motivated by concerns about denominational divisions, a belief that existing Christian groups did not reflect the "true church," and a desire to restore Christianity to what the original apostles had taught. Latter-day Saints consider both the Bible and *The Book of Mormon* to be Scripture, and they draw on a number of other writings like *Doctrine and Covenants* and *The Pearl of Great Price* to inform their faith as well. Latter-day Saints differ from traditional Christian groups by believing that the Father; his son, Jesus Christ; and the Holy Spirit are not one but three divine beings. The largest religious group from the Latter-day Saints movement is the Church of Jesus Christ of Latter-day Saints, whose headquarters is in Salt Lake City, Utah. Its organizational structure is highly centralized, starting with the Twelve Apostles, who guide the church's belief and practice. Regional districts are called *stakes*, and individual congregations are called *wards*. Members are assigned to attend a particular ward based on their address. Overseers in stakes (stake presidents) and wards (bishops) are men who have been chosen to provide leadership as volunteers. Although weekly worship occurs in wards, Latter-day Saints also worship in temples in which baptisms, weddings, and other special rituals take place. The Church of Jesus Christ of Latter-day Saints has grown significantly in recent decades and is known for its global missionary efforts. It's not very common in Alabama, though, with less than 1 percent of Alabamians belonging to the Church of Jesus Christ of Latter-day Saints.[6]

There are two possible reasons why relationships are so tight-knit among Churches of Christ and among Latter-day Saints wards. One reason is that these religious groups are both distinctive, strict, and theologically exclusive, and religious groups with these characteristics tend to have stronger within-group relational ties among their attenders. However, not every distinctive, strict, and theologically exclusive religious group in the network has such a tight-knit circle of relationships; the Southern Baptist, the Presbyterian Church in America, and even the Independent Fundamentalist congregations do not. Turning to the second rationale, I think that *restoration* is the key reason why relationships are so tight-knit within the Churches of Christ and the Church of Jesus Christ of Latter-day Saints. This theme—that the original church had been lost and needed to be restored—was central to the founding of the Restoration and Latter-day Saints movements. If a congregation thinks that only one (and its own) religious group truly represents Christianity, I can see why it might not just prioritize but exclusively develop relationships within its religious group.[7]

THE RICH SUPPORT OF TIES THAT BIND

Within tight-knit religious groups, theological similarity and close relationships can produce rich support, and congregations benefit from the emotional support, ideas, resources, and collaborations that they share in these relationships. However, the mechanisms for sharing support vary between Churches of Christ and Latter-day Saints wards because of differences in their organizational structures, so I discuss support within each group separately.

Churches of Christ

The Churches of Christ do not have a unifying creed or denominational organization, but there is significant theological similarity among them. Here's what two ministers said about the identity of the Churches of Christ.

> Within the Church of Christ, we are a relatively close-knit group, though we're all independent. We find a lot of commonalities because we all generally have a desire to follow the Bible as we read it, as we study it. In fact, there's an old saying from our history that says to speak where the Bible is speaking, to be silent where the Bible is silent. The differences are usually minor, like an order of worship or the style of songs that they sing.

The idea behind the Restoration movement and the Churches of Christ originally was, rather than reform what we consider the excesses of the Catholic Church, we would go back to the original pattern of the New Testament and simply be just Christians, which is why we refer to ourselves as nondenominational. We have a common ground to go back to, but we don't have a creed, a confession of faith, a synod, a convention, or anything like that. Each congregation is autonomous, completely under the leadership of elders. We're tied together by a strong belief in the plenary inspiration of the Scripture [that every word in the Bible is inspired by God[8]], and we use the expression of speaking where the Bible speaks and being silent where the Bible is silent. All of your belief systems are based on that, not a creed. Because of that, when we connect with each other and discuss back and forth, we have that common ground that tells us, whatever else we may disagree about, this is where the answer is going to be found.

The shared theological understandings provide a commonality around which these churches build tight-knit relationships.

These tight-knit relationships and high levels of trust among Churches of Christ are essential for building partnerships among autonomous congregations, and they also limit relationships with other religious groups. One minister explained,

Because we are independent and nondenominational—we don't have a denominational headquarters—those relationships are important because it builds those connections naturally and not forced by an overseer, so to speak. It's that natural friendship that works because we're all trying to do things similarly, and it encourages you when you see others that are doing similar things to keep doing what you're doing. It comes down to what we have adopted as core beliefs, even though we are without a headquarters. Some of those are things like how one actually obeys the death, burial, and resurrection of Christ and then a stand for worship—a cappella, without instruments—that limits your connections with other groups that would believe differently on those issues.

Another minister agreed. "It's a tight-knit community, and because there aren't connections with other religious traditions, I feel like that draws us even tighter to each other."

A minister shared a story that illustrates the high levels of trust and theological similarity among Churches of Christ.

Several years ago, I went to a conference in Chicago. I wanted to worship at a Church of Christ and found one in the yellow pages. I got a taxi to go to this congregation. It was on the south side of Chicago. I go in, and I'm the only Caucasian in the place. Everybody in there is African American. I go into Bible class. We start talking. We have a conversation. Everything's going well with the commonality of who we are and what we believe. After going back and forth in the Bible class, one of the men said, "You preach, don't you?" And I said, "Yes sir, as a matter of fact I do." He said, "Would you like to preach for us this morning?" I'm six hundred miles away from home in a congregation where I've never met anybody, but because we have that common background, that common history, and because we had talked and they knew the comments that I made in class, they felt comfortable to let me speak at their congregation without knowing anything else about me, other than "here's this white guy from Alabama."

This trust helps Churches of Christ to share ideas and resources and to collaborate.

Because Churches of Christ do not have an overseeing organization that can provide information and resources, it's largely up to local ministers to create an exchange between the churches. Tight-knit relationships have made it easy for Church of Christ ministers to brainstorm together about how to respond to the pandemic. One minister shared,

> We're all facing the same things as it applies to COVID—how we meet, when we meet. In the beginning of the pandemic, when we started realizing maybe it wasn't wise to meet together for a while, a lot of the churches went completely online. We talked about that, how we're going to make sure that we were able to reach people. [Another Church of Christ] had a parking lot worship service, and then we were talking about doing that here, so I reached out to [that minister] to say, "How'd y'all do it, how did you get the sound out to everybody, how did it work? With some people worried about contact, how do you . . . collect funds?" We talked about the fringe members that aren't showing up yet, how to reach out to them. A couple of us have gone to get coffee together and to have these conversations about how we're navigating it and bouncing ideas off each other. Is this working for you? Have you tried this? Well, this didn't work. Those types of things.

These tight-knit relationships are essential for sharing ideas and resources among autonomous Churches of Christ.

Tight-knit relationships among churches and leaders' trust in each other due to their theological similarity have also made it easy to build collaborations. The collaborations most commonly mentioned by ministers involved joint worship services, which have not taken place since the pandemic started. A minister described how, in one of these events,

> there were [a number of] congregations that participated. All of the preachers got together and talked about who we'd like to come to speak. We brought in a speaker from [another city in Alabama] who grew up at [a local] Church of Christ. Most of the preachers, we all knew him. He was a very dear friend of ours. We're noninstrumental, so all of the singing was a cappella. We had a

former youth minister from one of the area congregations who now lives in [another city in Alabama] come to lead the singing. Everybody knows [him]. So those relationships that are far-reaching tied us back together, so when we had this service, nobody worried about, "What if the preacher is going to say something I'm not going to like?" That commonality makes it very easy.

It's also been convenient for Churches of Christ to partner in other ways, with ministers preaching for each other if someone is sick, attenders partnering to do evangelism in their communities, and churches supporting and attending each other's revival services. Because of their tight-knit relationships, these churches have effectively partnered to organize events and collaborations and have not needed to rely on a denominational organization to do so.

The Church of Jesus Christ of Latter-day Saints

With its centralized leadership structure, the Church of Jesus Christ of Latter-day Saints can easily nurture tight-knit relationships and networks of support among leaders and attenders within a stake (a district) and local wards (congregations). There are close relationships among Latter-day Saints bishops, the men who lead wards as volunteers, within a particular stake. A leader described how

> these bishops come together and meet in meetings and in a training setting. In that time, they're discussing some of those challenges they're facing, and it becomes a bonding situation because one bishop will go, "What did you do with this situation? I've got something similar, and I'm wrestling with it. I'd like to know the best way to handle it." And you might have two to three other [ward] leaders go, "Well, I had a very similar situation. I did this." Someone else will say, "I did that." Someone else will say, "I did this." The bishop may or may not find something that was beneficial from what they said, but just the mere fact of being able to have that conversation opens the door for them to receive some promptings and some inspiration on how they can move forward in helping that individual or the circumstances they're dealing with.

These tight-knit relationships help bishops to share ideas and resources about how best to minister within their wards.

In addition, many people within wards get to know each other through stake-wide activities. These interactions can encourage tight-knit and supportive relationships between wards, and this support is particularly helpful in times of crisis. A Latter-day Saints leader explained,

> Because we do have interaction in all of these other activities, you really do get to know different people. When someone in one [ward] has a death in the family,

because of their interactions with other [wards], their friends are going to want to know. It may come to stake leadership, who then will send that information out to the different [wards]. "Just so you know, so and so passed away. Here's what we know about the funeral." Then the members of their own free will just want to reach out and say, "Hey, I'm here to support you." The traditional thing that most people do is, "Let me bring some food over." It's also because it's one of the tenets [of our faith] that we mourn with those that mourn. We feel like it's something to say, "Hey, you're not alone. We support you." The reality is we all end up going through something like that at some point in our lives, and we just really try to be a situation where people know you're never going to be alone. We're here to support you and help you to feel the love of the Savior.

Tight-knit relationships can produce many opportunities to provide and offer emotional support.

Latter-day Saints leaders seek to utilize their centralized structure to make experiences not only of worship and doctrine but also of friendship and support consistent across wards. A leader shared how

it doesn't matter where you go into, you're going to be worshipping the same way. You're going to be taught the same doctrine, and you're going to be loved and accepted—we hope—the same way. We want someone to be able to walk into [a ward] and feel the same wherever they went, so the resources are there to know that they can help each other, and a lot of the members know members from different units [wards], and there are friendships that have been developed over time.

Because of the tight-knit relationships among Latter-day Saints leaders and members, there are strong bonds of trust and emotional support.

Because the Church of Jesus Christ of Latter-day Saints is more centralized in its leadership structure, it can provide a broad range of resources to its leaders. A stake leader mentioned how he frequently talks with local bishops, shares resources with them, and points them toward other bishops to find help and advice. "We also train our bishops to help them understand the resources that the Church provides—and the Church provides extensive resources—both from leadership training and policies to where do you go to find counseling, to help these leaders to fulfill their calling. It's 100 percent, they're going to be able to find resources." The centralized structure of the Church of Jesus Christ of Latter-day Saints helped congregations to navigate worship during the pandemic. This leader shared,

About a year beforehand [before the pandemic started], the Church had introduced a program called Come, Follow Me, that Gospel teaching could take place in the home and should take place in the home. So when the pandemic hit, the announcement was that we have Come, Follow Me. You're expected to do it at home and make the home the center of your worship. The Church will support what takes place in the home by providing additional resources, using the Zoom platform and other things like that, so it really was very seamless.

Thanks to this new policy, Latter-day Saints leaders could use established resources to guide their wards through the pandemic without too much disruption to families' worship.

The Church of Jesus Christ of Latter-day Saints' organizational structure also makes it quite easy for wards to collaborate for community service. A leader described the following:

We get notifications that there's been a tornado or hurricane; if we're within a five-to-six-hour drive, we're going to get an invitation to gather our stake and members from each of the wards, and we'll go down and spend [a few] days. Generally, we have wards working with each other. That's one of the things we do quite frequently. We come together for one cause, to give service to people we know, people we don't know—it doesn't really matter. We're going to help our brothers and sisters.

The leadership structure helps Latter-day Saints to mobilize people effectively. "Because we do this all over the world, we have a good reputation. So when something [a disaster] hits, we can generally be some of the very first people allowed to start the recovery process. We can mobilize fairly quickly, and it's given us a great reputation."

Tight-knit relationships among wards also make it easy to collaborate in ministering to their members, and a leader mentioned an example related to events for teenagers. In 2021 wards across the stake returned to a pre-pandemic activity of "holding dances where the youth from each of the wards would come together and just have a good time dancing together. They want to do that because they want to mix and mingle with others from other units [wards], and some of them would bring their friends that weren't members of the church, and [they are] glad to have them come on along and enjoy." According to this leader, it's important for Latter-day Saints teenagers to have relationships across wards because having "like-minded beliefs makes it easier to feel like you're among an accepted group of friends." These collaborations among Latter-day Saints, which are easy to develop due to their relationships and their centralized leadership structure, allow them to pool resources and to expand their opportunities for ministry.

Rich Support across Different Organizational Structures

It's interesting how similar Churches of Christ and Latter-day Saints wards are in the rich relationships and support that they experience within their religious group, despite having opposite leadership structures. Each group's belief that it alone is the true restoration of the Christian church might explain why its congregations are bound together so tightly. Other religious groups with a variety of organizational structures may also be able to develop these tight-knit and supportive relationships *if* they believe that they are the only true approach to faith. However, these tight-knit relationships tend to be less common in other religious groups because many other religious groups are not as theologically exclusive.

DISADVANTAGES OF TIGHT-KNIT RELATIONSHIPS

Some Church of Christ and Latter-day Saints ministers, while grateful for the support they receive within their religious group, shared some downsides of these tight-knit circles of relationships, and three key disadvantages stood out in our conversations. "Ties that bind" can restrict congregations through discouraging innovation, questioning minor differences in approach, and making it more difficult to develop relationships with congregations from other religious groups.

Tight-knit clusters can create peer pressure that discourages innovation.[9] One of the Church of Christ ministers I talked with shared how his church has innovated by adding an instrumental service. This is a big deal in the Church of Christ because noninstrumental worship is understood by many Churches of Christ to be an essential part of their identity and doctrine. "We're not a typical Church of Christ. Our first service is a cappella; our second service is instrumental. We made the decision to go instrumental after many years of soul searching. We simply felt like, if we're going to reach [young adults] with what we believe, we need to be able to reach them, and Christian music is a very big part of their lives." The decision to innovate through adding an instrumental service has impacted relationships with nearby Churches of Christ, according to this minister. "Because of that, quite frankly, our relationships with other Churches of Christ locally are not as close as you may think they would be. We're not adversarial. It's simply we've gone a different path." This church's minister did not think relationships with other local Churches of Christ could provide helpful ideas or resources or that these relationships impacted how his congregation responded to opportunities and challenges. Having an instrumental service has also limited opportunities to partner with other local Churches of Christ. "Personally, it would be a breakthrough if we collaborated one-on-one with another Church of Christ here in [our community]." When looking for resources, this church reaches out to larger Churches of Christ outside the study area that have also added instrumental services. Because of the tight-knit relationships among local

Churches of Christ and the importance of noninstrumental worship for other local Churches of Christ, this congregation jeopardized support and opportunities to collaborate by innovating in its worship style.

Another concern about tight-knit relationships is that sometimes people can interfere in situations where they don't belong. A Church of Christ minister shared how he was counseling

> a family, a couple that was having some problems in their relationship. In trying to deal with that, things got back to another congregation where [the couple] had family, and the close, tight family situation was hard to deal with without ruffling feathers in two or three [churches]. That was one of the cases where you deal with it and then everybody else is, "Well, why are you doing it that way?" None of your business. You say that with Christian love, but everyone's in everyone else's business. It's almost like a small town.

This dynamic can also be problematic in areas where there are variations between Churches of Christ. This minister described how "if you decide to do something just a little bit different, which may or may not be book, chapter, and verse [tied to an explicit biblical passage], it may be an expedient, just a method of doing something, you may have somebody across town or in the next county over who says, 'Well, why are you doing it that way?'" Even in minor, non-doctrinal areas, tight-knit relationships can encourage conformity and limit variations in approach.[10]

Tight-knit relationships can also constrain congregations' ability to build relationships outside of their religious group.[11] A Latter-day Saints leader shared,

> If there are any boundaries, it's simply our own traditions of staying within because the reality is we would like [wards] to be more interactive with other religions. Some of it comes from the fact that some religions would have issues with some of our beliefs, and for some of our older members, there's no use going out and trying to work with other churches because they disagree with some of our doctrines and they've rebuffed us in the past. So it's easier for us to stay within our own world, but that's not the way we want it to be.

This leader described an opportunity to collaborate across religious groups and, in doing so, to find common ground. After some severe weather,

> we worked with [a nondenominational church] and had a great experience. In the past, they've been careful about wanting to do anything with us, but they came out and we worked with them. Afterward, they were like, "Hey anytime you guys want to work with us, we would love it. You guys brought tons of people. We had a great experience, it worked out really well." Very friendly. That's

just what we had hoped for. We weren't asking for anything other than to be a resource, to help when we can help, and to be part of the community as a whole.

However, if a congregation only develops relationships within its religious group because of negative past experiences with other religious groups, it loses opportunities to dispel stereotypes and to build rapport across religious groups,[12] which can contribute further to its isolation.

TIPS FOR YOUR CONGREGATION

If you are part of a distinctive, tight-knit religious group and would like advice about building relationships within your religious group, please look at the tips near the end of chapter 2.

RECAP AND NEXT STEPS

Relationships within distinctive religious groups that believe they are the only true approach to faith can be very tight-knit, even when the organizational structures of the groups are quite different. The theological similarity and strong relationships within these groups facilitate trust, emotional support, sharing of information and resources, and collaborations that can strengthen congregations' ministries for their members and in the community. However, these tight-knit relationships can also hinder innovation and isolate congregations from other religious groups.

In chapter 4, we turn to relationships between congregations from different religious groups. These relationships are not as common as relationships within religious groups, but they have pros and cons. They often provide congregations with a wider variety of ideas and resources as well as a wider range of opportunities for collaboration, but they take more intentionality to develop and tend not to be as strong as relationships within religious groups.

QUESTIONS TO CONSIDER

1. Are you part of a distinctive, tight-knit religious group where most congregations only have relationships within your religious group?
2. How did you develop these relationships?
3. What support have you offered or received through them?

4. How can you use insights from this chapter to create and strengthen relationships within your religious group?
5. How might these relationships help your congregation to navigate its opportunities and challenges and to support other congregations?

Chapter 4

Bridging Near and Far

Relationships between religious groups matter for how congregations navigate opportunities and challenges, and here's why. It's fairly common to learn about a rumor, a new idea, or an opportunity from an acquaintance before hearing about it from a close friend because our acquaintances tend to be in different social circles. These acquaintances can create bridges between social circles across which information and resources can spread more easily and rapidly, and people with more acquaintances tend to learn about new ideas and a wider range of opportunities more quickly.[1] This is true not only for individuals but also for congregations.

Because congregations within the same religious group tend to flock together, relationships between congregations from different religious groups are less common. Forty-three percent of the relationships in figure 4.1 (338 of 793) bridge across religious groups. These relationships are often less convenient for congregations to develop, but they provide valuable opportunities for congregations to learn about ideas and resources and to collaborate in ministry.[2] In their relationships that bridge between religious groups, theologically conservative congregations tend to connect to congregations from other theologically conservative religious groups (bridging near), while some liberal churches and non-Christian congregations partner despite significant theological differences (bridging far). This chapter focuses on how congregations build relationships between religious groups, the benefits of these relationships, how congregations use these relationships to navigate opportunities and challenges, and the disadvantages of these relationships.

BUILDING RELATIONSHIPS BETWEEN RELIGIOUS GROUPS

Because relationships between religious groups are not as convenient to develop as relationships within religious groups, congregations that seek to

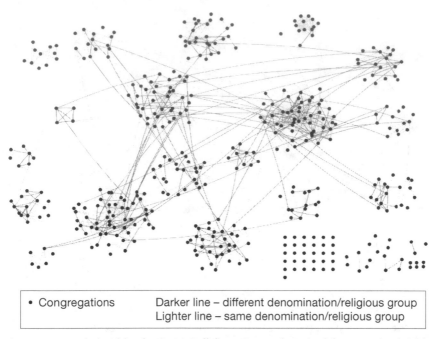

| • Congregations | Darker line – different denomination/religious group
Lighter line – same denomination/religious group |

Figure 4.1.   Relationships between Religious Groups in a Social Network of Central Alabama Congregations. Created by the author using NodeXL Basic (http://nodexl.code-plex.com) from the Social Media Research Foundation (https://www.smrfoundation.org).

build these relationships often need to be intentional about doing so. Here are three ways in which congregations can build relationships across religious groups.

1. Local ministerial associations provide opportunities to get to know congregations from a variety of religious groups and are typically organized around a neighborhood or municipality. "Some do little more than gather for an occasional lunch and schmoozing. Most, however, have a strong component of prayer and fellowship. . . . Often the praying is specifically directed at needs and concerns in the community, and the concerns expressed in prayer spill over into concrete actions the group may undertake."[3]

2. Congregations can also develop relationships between religious groups through informal relationships between their ministers. A minister at a nondenominational church in a small suburb of Birmingham is intentional about getting to know new ministers in his community regardless of their church's denominational affiliation (or lack thereof) and helping them to build relationships with other churches. "We tend to be

less thoughtful of trying to build our particular local church and more thoughtful about just adding to [God's] kingdom, whatever that looks like in our community, city, and region."

3. Relationships between attenders from different denominations can also encourage partnerships between their congregations. A Christian Methodist Episcopal minister shared, "Even though we were different denominations, we knew each other, our children went to the same schools, we all faced some of the same challenges, and we were able to build each other up. The African proverb says it takes an entire village to raise a child. Well, that village is made up of a community of congregations who have come together."

When congregations build relationships between religious groups, there is often a commonality that forms the basis of the relationship in the absence of a shared religious group. This commonality tends to differ between more theologically conservative congregations, which bridge near, and some more theologically progressive churches and non-Christian congregations, which bridge far.

Bridging Near

For many of the more conservative, Evangelical Protestant congregations, bridges across religious groups typically involve relationships with other conservative congregations, which are based on a shared understanding of the Gospel or Good News, a belief that God saves people from sin and death by bringing them into a relationship with Himself, typically through a short prayer. A small-town Southern Baptist minister described the importance of the Gospel for interdenominational relationships. "We're headed in the same direction biblically, and we're trying to focus on the essentials of the Gospel. I don't know if there would be that strong of a connection without it. It's not that we wouldn't get along, but I do think that we've got to have that to be able to partner and work together." A Presbyterian Church in America minister in Birmingham, whose church has a variety of interdenominational partnerships, agreed. "We're very well connected in the conservative Protestant, evangelical network of Jefferson County [where Birmingham is located], even beyond the PCA. [Our pastor is] very social and has championed [the congregation's] vision all across the country, and we've found a lot of like-minded, Gospel-centered partners." Conservative congregations tend to prioritize this theological similarity when building interdenominational relationships.

Focusing on the Gospel also helps these congregations to navigate differences in style and in doctrine across denominations and nondenominational groups. According to a nondenominational minister I interviewed,

> We may worship different, sound different, talk different, preach a little bit different, but if we're saying that we believe in the same God, the same Bible, then the common theme that's the nucleus of us all is Jesus. So if we're all together and believe in that one common theme, then I think how we do things and the way we do things wouldn't hinder us. That common theme allows us to be able to collaborate.

A shared conservative theology also helps congregations to respect each other in the areas where they have doctrinal differences. A minister from a predominantly African American Baptist church described his approach: "I don't go into a Methodist or a Pentecostal church and try to push Baptist doctrine on them, because they have their identity. I pull on the similarities that we all believe that Jesus is the Christ, the son of the living God, and we all believe that the Gospel is the Good News." When theologically conservative congregations build relationships across religious groups, it's often with congregations that are also theologically conservative and that share their understanding of the Gospel.

Bridging Far

More liberal churches and non-Christian congregations tend to collaborate around social justice, despite significant theological differences, and to nurture tolerance and respect for other religions. A suburban Cooperative Baptist Fellowship minister shared that his congregation's "faith model engenders respect for all persons. Therefore, we don't have folks acting in caustic ways toward other religious folk who are non-Christian." A pastor of a suburban United Methodist congregation described his church's faith formation for youth:

> We take them to one of the [Jewish] temples downtown to worship at a Shabbat service. We try and model tolerance, love, and acceptance of others while still clinging to what we feel like are the central tenants of the [Christian] faith. We've had Muslim scholars come and do panels here at the church, and it's not because we think Islam and Christianity are really the same. There are distinct and important differences between those faith traditions, but one of the tenants of our faith is the way we interact with those who are not like us.

A Muslim congregation intentionally builds relationships with congregations of other faiths who value religious diversity, with a leader seeing them as "a great resource because they have got uncles, aunts, and other relatives who may not know Muslims as well, so they can become an ambassador" to communicate appreciation for Islam and to dispel stereotypes about Islam. In my conversations, many ministers and leaders at theologically liberal churches and non-Christian congregations value religious diversity and encourage tolerance.

Common collaborations involve social justice and community activism in which there are shared goals despite theological differences. Many theologically progressive churches and non-Christian congregations in the Birmingham metro area have partnerships through Greater Birmingham Ministries, "a multi-faith, multi-racial organization that provides emergency services for people in need and engages the poor and the non-poor in system change to build a strong, supportive, engaged community and pursue a more just society for all people."[4] These congregations advocate and volunteer together around a variety of issues, including racial justice, support for the LGBTQ+ community, homelessness, access to medical insurance, and payday lending. Many of these congregations care deeply about social justice and focus on this commonality in building relationships between religious groups, despite significant theological differences.

BENEFITS OF RELATIONSHIPS BETWEEN RELIGIOUS GROUPS

Of the three types of support that I describe in chapter 1, two stood out in my conversations with ministers about relationships between religious groups. Compared to relationships within religious groups, it's not as convenient for congregations to share these types of support across religious groups, but these forms of support are often of better quality when shared between religious groups

Exchanging Ideas and Resources

When congregations are navigating opportunities and challenges, it's helpful to be able to brainstorm and to share ideas and resources with other congregations. Relationships between congregations from different religious groups are particularly beneficial because, compared to relationships within religious groups, they can expose congregations to a wider range of ideas and resources.[5] Here are two examples. An Eastern Orthodox priest shared how a wider range of ideas and resources is helpful for discerning how to minister amidst change. "Because we're all kind of in the same boat, we can examine the initiatives that [congregations from other religious groups have] taken and see and kind of get a lead, like this is working out really well for them, or this is going nowhere for them, and so it kind of saves us a little bit of trial and error." A predominantly African American Baptist congregation has also benefited from accessing a wider range of information. "It makes us more open, it gives us more ideas of what's going on, and it gives us an impetus to go out and do some things that, traditionally, we probably would not have done."

The ideas and resources congregations have found through relationships between religious groups have been helpful for navigating opportunities and challenges. A pastor of a nondenominational church in a small suburb of Birmingham said,

> Almost every church [in our suburb] has less than one hundred people, and so we all have the same issues with staffing, funding, and resources. That's one of the reasons that we're so intentional about working together to try to get things accomplished. My first response is always to partner with other churches, other pastors, [and] other ministries and organizations to see if, together, we can have more resources available and can accomplish more. Since we face some of the same things, we're able to encourage one another, speak to one another as to how one church has overcome this obstacle and maybe how we could overcome it utilizing the same things they did.

An African American Baptist minister also shared how reaching out to a nondenominational church for ideas and resources about hiring a church administrator was helpful for his well-being.

> I called [a nondenominational church] because I was trying to find out what a church administrator does, the kind of pressures they take off of the minister. I was able to talk with their church administrator as to what they do because, at that point, I was trying to take some of the pressure and some of the load off of me, so that was good to have an idea of what they do with their administrator.

These congregations found a wider range of ideas and resources through building relationships outside of their religious group.

Collaborations

There are also advantages for congregations that collaborate between religious groups. Although it's easier to collaborate within a religious group, collaborations between religious groups tend to be more effective because congregations can draw on a wider range of ideas, skills, and resources.[6] This has been particularly important for congregations who may not be able, on their own, to invest in as many ministry opportunities as they would like to. A Presbyterian Church (U.S.A.) congregation during the pandemic shared,

"We've definitely learned more about being able to share resources and ideas and to partner." And the congregation is "realizing we're not the only ones working on X, Y, or Z, and we don't have to be a leader on every issue either in the church or in society. If others are doing good work, we can partner with them, show up, and help them."

These collaborations between religious groups help congregations to pool their ideas, skills, and resources and to expand the ways in which they can minister. A United Methodist minister who has been limited in how he can minister to the LGBTQ+ community by denominational policies mentioned a valuable relationship with a local Presbyterian Church (U.S.A.) congregation. "With the LGBTQ rights issues that are still troubling our denomination, [the other church's minister] has more freedom with that area, so I've been able to reach out to her for some opportunities to refer people for ministry that's beyond what we're allowed to offer at this point." A Christian Methodist Episcopal minister also shared,

> when the Word of God [the Bible] talks about the Body of Christ [the Christian church]—that there are many members and they still make up the whole body— what becomes quite clear is that, while you might not have a particular resource or skill set in your congregation, it very well might be on the next corner or down the street. When we start bringing in those individuals who have those skill sets to maximize our ministry capacity, then we start seeing things really blooming and blossoming like God intended.

Partnering across different religious groups often strengthens the effectiveness of ministry collaborations because congregations can draw on a wider range of ideas, perspectives, and resources.

NAVIGATING OPPORTUNITIES AND CHALLENGES TOGETHER ACROSS RELIGIOUS GROUPS

There are many ways in which congregations are using relationships between religious groups to navigate opportunities and challenges, and here are some examples from theologically conservative churches, theologically progressive churches, and non-Christian congregations. As you read the profiles, I encourage you to notice in particular how relationships between religious groups impact congregations' ministry in their communities.

A Small-Town Southern Baptist Church

The mission of this Southern Baptist church is to love God and love people through worship, ministry within the congregation, and evangelism and outreach in the community. Its pastor described what this church's leadership wants and said, "To make sure across the board, whether in children's ministry or music ministry or whatever, that we're reflecting that mission in what we do. Of course, there are some things we do where we may not accomplish all of those things with a singular activity, but we try to make sure that that's instilled in what we do."

Relationships with other congregations from different religious groups have been helpful for navigating opportunities and challenges primarily related to changes in attendance and reaching out to the community during the pandemic. This pastor shared, "The challenges are to continue to engage people in serving and being active in the local church. While we've had some people that I'm not sure why they're not serving, we've had even more new people come along who are actively attending and wanting to be a part of the congregation." This church's minister has built relationships through "a smaller pastors' gathering that goes across denominational lines. There are a couple of [Southern] Baptist churches, a couple of ARC [Association of Related Churches[7]] churches, an independent Baptist church, and then another Presbyterian (PCA) church that . . . all network together, pray together, spend some time together."

These relationships between religious groups, according to this pastor, have helped this church to find a wider range of ideas and resources and to build collaborations. "We've bounced ideas off each other, and just even simple stuff like, 'Are you canceling church tonight?' Especially when we were canceling some things and doing live stream for a while, we were really talking a lot to each other about what we were trying, and trying to do some things at the same time and together for the sake of the community." This pastor described how, through these relationships, the churches have also been better able to minister in their community.

> We're agreed on the essentials of the Gospel and the scriptures. We're not going to bend on that, but we don't all have to worship exactly the same way and be just alike in what we do. I think that helps all of us to reach people in a more effective way because people are seeing these pastors, these churches, are unified over Christ. They're not unified over a denomination or peripheral things.

This church's outreach to the community is more effective because of its partnerships with congregations from other religious groups.

Another Small-Town Southern Baptist Church

This church's mission is oriented around a biblical verse, to "do all to the glory of God."[8] A pastor described how, when deciding on ministries, its ministers ask, "Does this glorify God? Is it for the building up of the church with the expansion of God's kingdom? Is the Great Commission being fulfilled [to teach others about Christ and baptize them], and are we making disciples [followers of Jesus]?" This church uses these questions to guide decisions about how it worships and engages in different ministries.

This church has experienced challenges related to the COVID-19 pandemic and opportunities to serve in its community. Its pastor shared, "Like most churches post-COVID, we're trying to get back to where we were pre-COVID. Make no mistake, it affected everybody as far as numbers, as far as people feeling comfortable with assimilating back to church." This church has been able to serve people in need in its community through a local inter-denominational ministerial association. This pastor explained,

> We have a very strong ministerial association in [our county] that cuts across denominational lines. We may have differences of opinion and disagreements doctrinally, and we may have differences in certain roles that people should play or certain approaches to ministry, but when it comes to ministering as effectively as possible to the community, we're pretty strong in that.

Through this association, churches can pool their resources in order to serve more effectively in the community. This Southern Baptist church hosts a weekly counseling service that anyone in the community can reach out to, and the churches in the ministerial association also collaborate to serve and provide assistance for people who are experiencing homelessness in their community. This ministerial association has allowed this Southern Baptist church to minister in the community in ways that it could not have alone.

A United Methodist Congregation in a Suburb of Birmingham

This church has a strong focus on ministering in its community. According to its minister, it "sees itself as a missional congregation. [They] want to be a blessing to [their] community, not just to [their] church members." This church also seeks to create an inclusive environment "where unchurched folks are welcome and people on the margins of faith find a place in the life of the church." This minister shared how relationships are central to this church's identity: "Ultimately, you can have tremendous faith and perfect doctrine, but if you're not practicing love of neighbor and love of God, it's a waste of time."

This congregation shared opportunities and challenges related to the COVID-19 pandemic and cultural polarization. The first involves online outreach during the pandemic. Its minister explained, "We are reaching more people on paper than we ever have before because of online presence, but frankly, I don't know who is in my church anymore. We're getting prayer requests, doing online discipleship, and getting even pledge [financial giving] cards from people that have never set foot in our building." The second concerns the impact of political and theological polarization within the congregation. The minister describes this congregation as valuing

> justice for the poor and full inclusion of [people who are] LGBTQ. Methodist churches tend to be a very big tent, and [the congregation] really straddles the American political spectrum. Having a broad base of political and theological views in one community that has a shared mission is becoming more and more difficult, so I think the politicization of faith is a huge challenge.

A friendship with a minister of a Baptist church has been very helpful for sharing ideas during the pandemic. "We always check in with each other. There were several months where we were talking once a week to figure out what to do next." This church also values collaborating with congregations from different religious groups to advocate for social justice. This minister shared, "We're less likely to focus on the things that distinguish us than we are to focus on the things that bind us together, particularly relative to people living in poverty, social justice issues, and practical faith. A lot of times, when you are sharing in an action, it's much easier to get over differences in beliefs." These collaborations across religious groups have strengthened this church's impact in the community because "we all have different gifts, and we all bring different things to the table."

A Muslim Congregation in Birmingham

This congregation seeks to provide holistic services to the Muslim community in Birmingham, including worship, social needs, marriages, and funerals, as well as practical support like help finding a job or seeking resources in the community. A leader there explained, "We are a resource for the print and the electronic media about anything that happens in the Muslim world. We are the resource to answer those questions. So we definitely want to become the spokesperson of our faith, politically and religiously." This congregation also values charitable engagement and has developed partnerships with a variety of local community organizations.

This Muslim congregation's main opportunities and challenges concern its ministry to youth, advocating for social justice, and experiencing some prejudice and discrimination in the community. This congregation desires to strengthen its connection with its teenage attenders and has had conversations with congregations from other faith traditions to gather ideas and resources about starting a summer camp. It collaborates with congregations from other religious groups to address needs in the community and to work toward social justice through Greater Birmingham Ministries and some organizations serving people experiencing homelessness. Interfaith relationships are also quite valuable when this congregation faces prejudice and discrimination. It intentionally builds relationships with congregations of other faiths who value religious diversity and whose attenders can communicate appreciation for Islam, dispel stereotypes about Islam among friends and family members, and support the Muslim community when it experiences discrimination. Within the past decade, the Alabama Board of Education considered a request from a conservative group to ban books that presented Islam positively from the curriculum. A leader described how this situation played out: "When we became aware of that demand to ban those books, we were able to reach out to our diverse group of college professors and spiritual leaders, and there was a series of letters that went to the Alabama Board of Education, and they finally ended up not banning those books."[9] This Muslim congregation has nurtured relationships with and been supported by congregations from other religious groups.

A Jewish Congregation in Birmingham

A leader shared how this congregation ministers to a wide range of attenders, including those who are "less traditional to more traditional" as well as "observant to less observant. Because we're a relatively small Jewish community [in Birmingham], there are not so many options here, [compared to] being part of a Christian community here in Birmingham, where you can sort of choose your flavor." In addition, "Judaism means different things to different people, so some people's primary point of contact with Judaism is religious. The question for us is how we provide for the other points of access that people are looking for, whether it is social opportunities or whether it is engaging with Jewish culture and history." According to this leader, its mission is centered around "*Tikkun Olam*, which means repairing the world, and so we try to manifest that in our work, while also serving as a center of Jewish life for our congregants that offers them all different types of fulfillment from spiritual to social to cultural." This leader shared how the congregation also draws on *Tikkun Olam* to inform its advocacy in the community, about which it tries to be very discerning. "We're a pretty purple congregation politically.

In some of our social action work, we have to tread a line of not alienating anybody. It's difficult to be everything to everyone, and it's also necessary."

This congregation has extensive partnerships and collaborations with congregations of other faith traditions, particularly through an interfaith organization in its neighborhood. These relationships have helped congregations to share ideas and resources, to collaborate, and to advocate for each other more effectively. This leader shared,

> We did a great interfaith Thanksgiving [event] last year [in 2020], where a person filmed clergy solo in all their different congregations. We also had a joint prayer for people our communities have lost in COVID. As soon as we pitched the idea in an email to our core group, somebody had volunteered to videotape. Other people were throwing out suggestions about liturgy and what the service could look like. It was pretty easy to get the ball rolling on brainstorming that idea and bringing it to life.

These relationships between religious groups have been particularly valuable when Jewish communities have experienced a threat or discrimination. This leader described how "after the Pittsburgh shooting [at the Tree of Life synagogue in 2018], there was a pretty large interfaith rally and vigil, and we felt really supported by our interfaith communities." In addition, decades ago, "there was an attempt to bomb the synagogue. It luckily rained, and the dynamite didn't go off, but there was a reward put out to find the person who did it." In the congregation's bulletins at that time, "they printed all these letters from different faith organizations here in town. Even during a time where Jews were a little less accepted generally, other faith communities rallied to contribute to that reward pool." These interfaith relationships have provided this congregation with a broader range of resources, opportunities for ministry, and support.

A Presbyterian Church (U.S.A.) Congregation in Tuscaloosa

This church is quite theologically liberal and politically active, according to its minster:

> We are a progressive church. We aren't afraid to engage in conversations of faith and science or how we live out our faith in the political world. We're kind of out there on the left side of things. We are an internationally diverse community with regard to gender and an open and affirming congregation. We seek to be more racially diverse, and we do a lot of conversations around race and what that means for us as a congregation. We're a very politically engaged

congregation that seeks to continue to learn and grow our understanding of how the Bible influences our daily life.

This church invites LGBTQ+ groups and addiction support groups to meet in its building, and, according to its minister, it desires "to make sure that we engage in both advocacy work as well as trying to meet current needs." It offers a food pantry that feeds hundreds of families a month, and it is planning to add a community garden. When I interviewed this church's minister, this church had not yet returned to in-person services but was planning to do so soon.

This PC(USA) church has numerous relationships across religious groups, and these relationships have helped with navigating changes during the pandemic and with identifying opportunities to engage in its community. Its minister shared how "it's been helpful during the pandemic to have other pastors, to have conversations and to say, 'Well, what are you doing? When are you going to open? How are you handling X, Y, and Z? What are you going to do about music?' Knowing that we all want to do what's smart, safe, and compassionate, it's been helpful and comforting to go through this together." This minister described how this church has also been able to collaborate with other progressive congregations in its community service and advocacy.

> It's good to know that there are other congregations that are going to show up for things, to know that we're not going to be alone if we show up to the MLK Day march. We know that [a Unitarian Universalist congregation] is going to be there, and we can expect folks from [an Episcopal congregation] to be there. When a group of us got together to work on a no-interest microloan program, the resources around the table from the different congregations have been so helpful, the different skills and gifts that people bring, so just the pooling of resources to build and make things happen that we couldn't do on our own is very life giving.

Relationships with congregations from different religious groups have helped this church to access a wider range of ideas for how to worship during the pandemic and to expand its resources for advocacy in its community.

A Christian Methodist Episcopal Church in Birmingham

This church is a predominantly African American Methodist church, and its pastor described how it desires to "teach and reach the community of God with love and discipleship." This church uses "a mix of traditional and contemporary worship" because "we are a mixture of children, youth, young adults, young married couples with children, and senior citizens." This church is very active in serving its community, and it has a 501(c)(3) that seeks to support young people and their families.

This church's main challenges involve ministering via technology during the pandemic, and its main opportunities are related to community engagement. Its minister shared, "Our challenges are basically technology. We're trying to make sure that we set up platforms—Facebook, Zoom, and YouTube—to make sure that we maintain contact with our members and continue to do worship opportunities for the community." This church also partners with a nearby elementary school to provide tutoring for students. Relationships with congregations from other denominations have helped this church to make sure that it is not duplicating services that are already in the community, to expand its awareness about community ministry opportunities, to find resources for its nonprofit, and to build collaborations for community service. Its minister shared, "I befriend other pastors, whether it be a predominantly white congregation or another denomination, wherever I can find information that would be helpful for my congregation to grow and start to look into doing a new ministry. I have no problem with doing that if it's someone that can help us or show us something different to do." This church also partners with Faith in Action Alabama,[10] a social advocacy organization that has provided opportunities to collaborate across religious groups to address community issues and has provided resources around generating grant funding for this church's nonprofit. This minister was grateful to partner with other churches "during the pandemic [that] were doing food ministry, and [we] worked with them because it was something to help the community that was very needy. It wasn't about [our church], but it was about the community's needs and getting those needs met during this very tragic time in people's lives." Through collaborating with congregations from other religious groups, this church has been able to minister in its community more effectively.

A Roman Catholic Parish in Birmingham

According to its priest, this parish is "a small, vibrant community that gets most of its mission and identity beyond that which is common to any Catholic parish—from its social apostolates [its ministry in the community]. It's serving in a desperately poor neighborhood." This parish offers a variety of services to its community, including food, clothing, and after-school programs. The COVID-19 pandemic impacted the need for these resources. The priest described what happened: "We had, going into the pandemic, one of the larger food ministries in Birmingham. We served exclusively in [our zip code]. The pandemic and the associated economic instability just took the brackets off in who was coming to us [from outside our zip code] and just skyrocketed the need."

Relationships with congregations from other religious groups have supported this parish's commitment and ability to serve in its community. Its priest elaborated and said,

> We enjoy social ministry collaboration, and there is also just a sense of mutual affection. There are different traditions, different perspectives, and yet we're still sharing some common commitments, particularly around urban ministry. What we have in common isn't so much a theological core commitment but a hermeneutic of generosity toward each other. We have a diverse stream of pragmatic partners, even if we don't fully understand their traditions or context.

This priest also shared how this parish's openness to theological diversity has strengthened its relationships across religious groups.

> I don't know that we are at all interested in any sense of ideological purity. We have been described as a rogue Catholic sect, and so we might just be looking for peers who are outliers within their own denominations and traditions. In a lot of ways, we swap some notes about how we inform our home denomination or tradition [about community organizing[11] and ministry] and why we think this is so important, so we're looking for a sense of solidarity there.

Relationships between religious groups have allowed this congregation to build collaborations that support its urban ministry efforts.

A DISADVANTAGE OF RELATIONSHIPS BETWEEN RELIGIOUS GROUPS

Relationships between religious groups tend not to be as strong as relationships within religious groups. If you've read chapters 2 and 3, you might have noticed that, when I discussed the benefits of relationships between religious groups earlier in this chapter, I did not mention close, trusting relationships. Relationships that involve a similarity tend to be stronger, while relationships across differences tend to be weaker.[12] In our conversations some ministers gave examples of how relationships across religious groups are not as strong.

Some ministers from more theologically conservative religious groups shared how denominational differences have hindered some relationships and partnerships. A minister from a Presbyterian Church in America congregation described his experience in a previous ministry setting and said, "I tried so hard to unite myself with other brothers and sisters in Birmingham from different denominations, and generally, it went very well, but it always came down to us feeling like the outsider because you guys believe in pre-destination, you guys baptize babies, you guys sprinkle, you don't immerse." Similarly, a minister at an Independent Fundamentalist church encountered challenges when trying to collaborate on a ministry for men with nearby Southern Baptist churches.

> If you look at the Southern Baptists, we would tend to be doctrinally along the same lines, but they tend to be more inclined to rub shoulders with their own ilk. That may have been part of the deal with our meeting [about the partnership] where nobody really responded because the other churches that had pastoral staff attend [the meeting] were all Southern Baptist churches.

A predominantly African American Baptist church also mentioned difficulty maintaining denominational diversity in a joint community service endeavor. "With an outreach that started off being more multidenominational, we had to work really hard to keep the nondenominational churches involved. It seemed like all of the Baptist pastors really came together and were willing to work together, and some of the nondenominational pastors may have felt that this is more of a Baptist initiative." Despite shared conservative theology, denominational differences can result in weaker relationships.

Ministers and leaders from minority religious groups, which tend to have more interfaith partnerships with theologically progressive congregations, are also mindful that these relationships have limitations. The Muslim leader whose congregation I profiled above shared that his congregation differs from more progressive Christian churches in their views on morality. "When it comes to some of the liberal issues in the social and the moral environment, then we can kind of just part our ways. We just don't see eye-to-eye in this. Our stand for or against abortion or homosexuality is different." However, he added, "We don't let those differences come in our way because we still want to work for the social justice of everybody." A leader at the Jewish congregation I also profiled earlier in this chapter has some difficulty collaborating with more liberal churches on social advocacy because of the range of political and religious perspectives in the congregation. "There are a few folks [in our interfaith organization] who are more explicitly progressive Christian organizations," where advocating around social issues "might be less of a challenge because they're connecting on progressive political causes in a way that we're not, because of our political limitations." There are also boundaries around the extent to which an Eastern Orthodox congregation can partner across religious groups. "The engagement we have with [other congregations] is pretty much only in social justice issues, which deemphasize creed and emphasize common action. We cooperate mainly in terms of homelessness and poverty. We're limited basically to social justice issues of common concern, which is very ecumenical. We never get into any kind of issues of belief." Even for congregations that value interfaith relationships, these relationships are often weaker because of differences in beliefs, ethics, and political views.

TIPS FOR YOUR CONGREGATION

If you're a minister or leader and you'd like to build relationships across religious groups, here are some practical tips.

- Because many relationships between religious groups still have some type of commonality, think about what beliefs, practices, or values you would like to share in a relationship. It could be a more conservative or liberal theological approach, a commitment to evangelism or to social justice, a particular worship style, or something else.
- Explore whether there is an interdenominational or interfaith ministerial association already in your neighborhood or community. If there is, reach out to its leaders to learn more, and attend a few gatherings to see if it is a good fit for your congregation.
- If there's not a ministerial association in your community, you're not out of luck. Reach out to ministers and leaders at nearby congregations that you think might share the commonality that you value. See if you can get together for coffee or a meal to start to build a relationship.
- You can also ask your attenders about the congregations that their friends and family members attend. These friendships between attenders can form the basis for a strong relationship between the congregations. Reach out to ministers at these congregations, and seek opportunities to get to know them.
- Be intentional about building and maintaining these relationships. They're not as convenient to develop, and they tend to need regular contact to maintain them.

RECAP AND WHAT'S NEXT

In their relationships with congregations from other religious groups, theologically conservative congregations tend to bridge near with other theologically similar congregations, while progressive churches and some non-Christian congregations tend to bridge far across theological differences to advocate for social justice. Relationships between religious groups are very beneficial for congregations that are seeking ideas and resources for navigating opportunities and challenges because they allow information and ideas to spread more quickly. These relationships also tend to make collaborations more effective because of the broader range of ideas and resources that congregations can draw on. However, compared to relationships within religious groups, relationships between religious groups tend not to be as strong, and they require more intentionality to develop.

In chapter 5, we explore relationships between congregations that share the same racial composition. These relationships are very common among congregations, but it was hard to get many of the ministers and leaders I interviewed to talk about them. I use what I can from these conversations as well as some other resources to describe why relationships within racial groups are so common, some dynamics that make it difficult for congregations to build relationships beyond their racial group, and the ways in which these barriers impact congregations and reinforce racial divisions in central Alabama. This chapter has a different structure than what you've seen so far, and it focuses less on navigating opportunities and challenges because of ministers' hesitance to talk about these relationships.

QUESTIONS TO CONSIDER

1. How many of the congregations on your list are from a different religious group?
2. How did you develop these relationships?
3. What support have you offered or received through them?
4. How can you use insights from this chapter to create and strengthen relationships with congregations from different religious groups?
5. How might these relationships help your congregation to navigate its opportunities and challenges and to support other congregations?

Chapter 5

Racial Barriers

Racial divisions are fairly common in the United States, and it may not be surprising for you that they exist among congregations as well. Among individuals, many people prefer friends and romantic partners that share their race. People also tend to work and to learn in settings that don't have much racial diversity. Many neighborhoods are racially segregated to where it's not as common to have neighbors from different racial groups, and many people also worship in congregations with very little racial diversity.[1]

These racial divisions also impact relationships between congregations. Most congregations only or primarily interact with congregations that have the same racial composition. Figure 5.1 illustrates how relationships are more common between racially similar congregations, and 70 percent of the relationships in this diagram (557 of 793) are between congregations that share the same racial composition. It's safe to say that congregations of a feather flock together not only when they share the same religious group but also when they share the same racial composition. However, although many ministers and leaders were happy to share about their relationships within their religious group, it was difficult to get them to talk much about relationships with racially similar congregations and about how these relationships influence how they navigate opportunities and challenges. This was particularly true for ministers and leaders of predominantly non-Hispanic white congregations. Perhaps they were cautious about discussing this because of Alabama's history surrounding racial inequality.

In this chapter, I focus less on how these relationships help congregations to navigate opportunities and challenges and instead describe three barriers to relationships between congregations with different racial compositions. These barriers make relationships within racial groups easy and convenient to develop and encourage tight-knit relationships within racial groups, but they reinforce racial divisions in central Alabama.

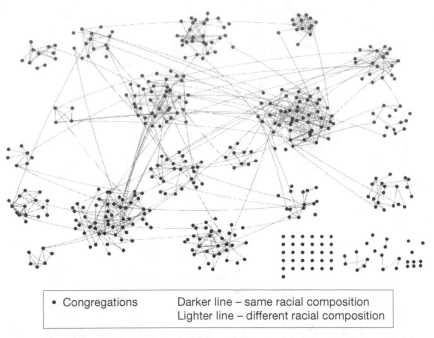

| • Congregations | Darker line – same racial composition |
| | Lighter line – different racial composition |

Figure 5.1.   Relationships within Racial Groups in a Social Network of Central Alabama Congregations. Created by the author using NodeXL Basic (http://nodexl.codeplex.com) from the Social Media Research Foundation (https://www.smrfoundation.org).

BARRIERS BETWEEN CONGREGATIONS FROM DIFFERENT RACIAL GROUPS

None of the congregational ministers and leaders I spoke with expressed any opposition to building relationships with congregations that have different racial compositions, but many shared that they tended not to because it was easiest to build relationships with similar congregations. One minister said that "we seek to be diverse, but at the same time, we tend to gravitate toward those that are like us." There are three barriers that make it more challenging and less convenient for congregations to build relationships with congregations from different racial groups.

Racially Homogeneous Religious Groups

The first barrier involves a lack of racial diversity in most religious groups. Most congregations have relationships primarily with congregations from their religious group because these relationships are often the most convenient to develop (see chapters 2 and 3). When congregations share the same religious group, they also tend to share the same racial group because most religious groups in the United States draw ministers, leaders, and attenders primarily from one racial group. In other words, congregations within the same religious group are likely to have the same racial composition as well. Among the central Alabama congregations that have participated in my research, about 70 percent are in religious groups where at least 80 percent of congregations have the same racial composition. So, because it's more convenient to build relationships within a congregation's religious group, it's also going to be convenient to build relationships within a congregation's racial group because of racial similarity within religious groups.[2]

These dynamics create a barrier for building relationships with congregations that have different racial compositions. Building a relationship with a congregation from a different racial group tends to involve building a relationship with a congregation from a different religious group as well, and these relationships are less convenient and take more effort and intentionality to develop. This barrier can thwart congregations that want to build more racially diverse connections.

Racially Segregated Neighborhoods

The second barrier is related to many congregations' tendency to build relationships with congregations in their local community. In fact, relationships are more common when there is a shorter geographic distance between the congregations. This tendency, however, creates a barrier to building relationships with congregations that have different racial compositions because of Alabama's history of racial segregation. It's been enshrined in the 1901 Alabama Constitution, and Alabama voters just voted to remove it in November 2022. Racial residential segregation may no longer be enforceable by law, but Figure 5.2 shows how it is still largely the reality in central Alabama. The average congregation that participated in my 2017–2018 survey is in a Census tract in which 80 percent of residents have the same race. Because many communities in central Alabama are segregated by race, when congregations build relationships with nearby congregations, they're likely to be with congregations that have the same racial composition.[3]

Some ministers and leaders of predominantly white congregations mentioned these dynamics to explain why they do not have many connections with congregations of color. One described how a local interfaith organization

> has been one of our primary ways of connecting with other congregations, and so we've had some discussions about the fact that, in Birmingham, one of the big challenges that we face as a city is the physical segregation of white and non-white communities. Because we've been operating in this [local

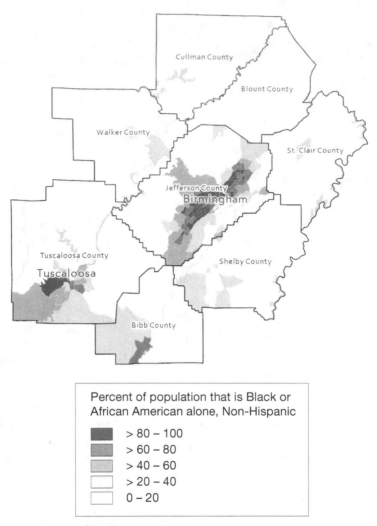

Percent of population that is Black or
African American alone, Non-Hispanic

■ > 80 – 100
▨ > 60 – 80
▨ > 40 – 60
□ > 20 – 40
□ 0 – 20

Figure 5.2. Racial Residential Segregation in Central Alabama by Census Tract. Created by the author using ArcGIS with assistance from Jonathan Fleming.

organization], it really limits our opportunity to connect with non-white faith communities, which is something we would like to do.

A minister at a congregation located in a small town that is predominantly white shared similar thoughts. "We reflect the community, which is not diverse at all. I would love to partner with congregations that are more diverse, and I have struggled to find ways to do that." Predominantly white congregations are not the only ones impacted by these dynamics.

Congregations of color also experience barriers to building relationships with predominantly white congregations because of neighborhood segregation. An African American Baptist minister shared about how relationships within predominantly African American neighborhoods encourage relationships between African American congregations.

> We're in a predominantly Black area, and our members typically don't travel far distances to go to church, so the neighborhoods feed into our churches. We have people in the community who are next-door neighbors, but one neighbor may go to this church, and the other neighbor may go to the next church, but there's still that connection there because they're next-door neighbors, they live in the same city, and they worship in the same city, just two different churches. So there's that kind of inter-woven connectivity.

This residential segregation can make it difficult for congregations of color to partner with predominantly white congregations. Another African American minister shared how "in this context where we're geographically located, there aren't a whole lot of, well there are white congregations around us, but they're in the rural and suburban areas. They are not in the inner city. There are one or two, but there's this disconnect. There has not been an intentional effort to come together." Because of this residential segregation, when predominantly African American congregations seek to collaborate with other congregations in their neighborhood, the collaboration mainly involves other predominantly African American congregations. Racially homogeneous neighborhoods are a barrier to building relationships with congregations that have different racial compositions for both white congregations and congregations of color.

Cultural Barriers

The third barrier to relationships between congregations with different racial compositions is related to cultural differences between racial groups. Here's how a minister from a predominantly African American nondenominational church described them.

> There are a lot of cultural differences that hinder relationships from happening. I think that, even from a race standpoint, that hinders those relationships from being established. I have pastor friends that I talk to that I know that the relationship probably can't be fostered any more, just because it's not what he may be thinking but it's what he thinks that his congregation may think if you establish a relationship outside of your race, outside of your culture.

In my research, when ministers mentioned racial and cultural barriers between congregations, they most commonly were between Black Protestant and white Evangelical Protestant churches. African American ministers were the most likely to talk about these barriers, and they described three types—theological, political, and pandemic-related—that impede relationships.

Starting with theological barriers, white Evangelical congregations tend to emphasize "that Christ died for the salvation of all, and that anyone who accepts Christ as the one way to eternal life will be saved." Black Protestants don't necessarily disagree, but they more strongly emphasize freedom, justice, liberation, and deliverance. In their engagement in the community, Evangelicals tend to focus more on evangelism, while Black Protestants have higher levels of volunteering and community engagement. According to an African American pastor, these differences create barriers to relationships between Evangelical and Black Protestant churches.

> Our theological foundations are different. They preach more of a white, evangelical message, dealing specifically with salvation, and I deal with it, but I deal with the fact that you've got to live in hell on earth. What many of them have come to discover during COVID is that people don't want to hear about heaven; they want to hear about where I can go get my vaccination. With you so focused on heaven, you ain't talking about vaccinations, where I can go and get food for my family.

Because of these theological differences, some African American ministers are concerned when predominantly white congregations move into their neighborhoods. "Some [pastors] believe that, in their community, you need to stay out of it, so there are territorial fights that take place among certain pastors about people coming into their community, their neighborhood trying to establish something." When a predominantly white multisite megachurch started a location at a local high school, "it didn't work. A lot of pastors absolutely let it be known that you are not welcome in this community." These theological barriers can limit relationships and partnerships between Black and Evangelical Protestant congregations.[4]

There are also political differences between Evangelical and Black Protestants that can hinder relationships. Many Evangelicals in central Alabama are politically conservative, while many Black Protestants are more politically progressive. Because so many attenders at Evangelical churches supported former President Trump, who has inflamed racial tensions throughout the country, some ministers and leaders at predominantly African American congregations expressed concerns about developing relationships with predominantly white congregations due to differing views on racial inequality and justice. Here's what a minister of a predominantly African American Baptist church said.

> The events that took place on January 6 [2021] and then, going back to 2020, Black Lives Matter and all of those things that surfaced—the murders of Black men by police officers and things like that—there is a strong tension between Black and white pastors. African American congregations by and large are Democratic politically, and the white congregations are going to be very conservative in nature. When we read Scripture, our interpretations are different from one another, and so our approach to this COVID crisis, our approach to January 6 or what happened with Black Lives Matter in 2020, we have very different views. Since the rise of all of these current events, there are African American pastors saying that we're not going to have any more conversations with white pastors about Christianity and religion.

Cultural polarization, particularly surrounding racial injustice, can make it difficult for Black and Evangelical Protestant congregations to build relationships.[5]

Another barrier to relationships between congregations with different racial compositions involves how the congregations have responded to the COVID-19 pandemic. Communities of color have been more adversely impacted by the pandemic and have expressed greater concerns about catching COVID and spreading it to others. Because of this, Black Protestant congregations have been less likely to return to in-person gatherings, and this makes partnering with white Evangelical congregations that are less likely to observe public health guidelines more difficult. An African American Baptist minister shared that

> we're all trying to determine how to do ministry in this COVID context, and so every pastor and congregation that I've spoken with among African Americans particularly are concerned about in-person gatherings. Thinking about the African American and the white churches in this area, there's so much tension. There's a vast difference. Black congregations are going to be masked up, and we're going to be overly cautious of COVID, whereas I have noticed that pastors of the white churches are unmasked and they're back in full swing. Everybody can come, and the distance and all of those things are out, so that is a big difference.

Concerns about getting or spreading COVID can discourage African American congregations and their ministers from building partnerships and relationships with white congregations who have returned to pre-pandemic patterns of worship and activities.[6]

There are many barriers to building connections between congregations of different racial compositions. Some involve tendencies to build relationships within racially homogeneous religious groups and within racially segregated neighborhoods, while others concern differences in theology, politics, and responses to the pandemic.

CONVENIENCE AND SOLIDARITY

Because of these barriers, it's much more convenient to build relationships within racial groups. Some research about dynamics that discourage racial diversity within congregations can shed light on why. On an individual level, people tend to prefer relationships with people who share their same race, and this preference often means that people prefer to attend congregations that primarily consist of people with the same racial background. This racial similarity creates a more distinct identity for the congregation, clearer boundaries around who belongs in the congregation, and a greater sense of solidarity and community within the congregation. It also makes it easier for attenders to find meaning and belonging in their congregation. In multiracial congregations, attenders are more likely to raise concerns that the congregation isn't meeting their needs or reflecting their preferences. Many congregations have found that it's easier to cater just to one racial group instead of adapting their ministry to reflect a wider range of cultures, life experiences, and preferences. For congregations, it's also easier and takes less effort and intentionality to build relationships with congregations that have the same racial composition.[7]

The solidarity in racially homogeneous relationships can be particularly helpful for congregations of color whose ministers, leaders, and attenders are more likely to experience inequality, prejudice, and discrimination. For decades, predominantly African American churches have provided a safe space for their attenders and leaders to worship and to pursue opportunities that may not be available to them in predominantly white congregations. Here's what Franklin Frazier, the first African American sociologist to be elected president of the American Sociological Society (now Association), said in the 1960s:

> In providing a structured social life in which the Negro could give expression to his deepest feeling and at the same time achieve status and find a meaningful existence, the Negro church provided a refuge in a hostile white world. . . . The Negro church with its own forms of religious worship was a world in which the white man did not invade. . . . Since the Negro was not completely insulated from the white world and had to conform to some extent to the ways of white men, he was affected by their evaluation of him. Nevertheless, he could

always find an escape from such, often painful, experiences within the shelter of his church.

Relationships among congregations of color can also create a safe space for sharing support, exchanging ideas and resources, and collaborating.[8]

Some ministers who lead congregations of color shared about the support they've experienced in this safe space. A priest at a multiracial Catholic parish in a predominantly African American neighborhood described how this safe space encourages trust. "The social context, economic context of our neighborhoods effectively means we're all in the same foxhole. So to mix the metaphors, there's a lot of trust for the person next to you and significantly less trust the farther away you get from that foxhole. So I think that our social and demographic context is one where we have a lot of solidarity." An African American Baptist pastor shared how this safe, trusting environment helps congregations to be able to share ideas and resources.

> We are all in the same city. We realize that we're all facing the same kind of situation and we are all trying to move forward. We are all trying to figure out how to connect with Millennials. We are all trying to figure out how to keep our churches open post-COVID. What we've done is formed this alliance. Let's continue to try to gather resources so that we can keep each other informed and work together to make sure that our churches thrive and are alive and vibrant on the other side of the pandemic.

This safe space also nurtures partnerships. An African American nondenominational minister explained how, when ministering in the community, racial "similarities do help us to collaborate because we do have some sort of a common goal, a common challenge that we all are familiar with. It is something that helps us to find a common ground when we get a chance to sit down and talk." Racially homogeneous relationships can provide congregations of color with support that's less likely to be impacted by racial prejudice.

These relationships can be quite valuable when people at congregations of color experience racial discrimination. An African American Baptist pastor described how a fellow African American pastor

> had a very aggressive experience with a police officer in a neighboring town. I went with the pastor to his meeting with the police chief, who was the one following up on the assault, and he [the police chief] started out with, "I don't see color," but then he was like, "I want to do the right thing." Well, let's start here. Don't ever tell anybody that you don't see color because you erase who they are. So we had to come from the theological position of the imago Dei [image of God] in order to be able to say that color is not sinful, melanin pigmentation is not sinful. We have to stop treating it as if it is something that is negative

or bad. He [the police chief] had no sphere of understanding until we had that conversation with him.

In this situation, strong relationships between local African American pastors helped them to be able support and advocate for their colleague who experienced discrimination.

REINFORCING RACIAL DIVISIONS

However, racially homogeneous relationships can also exacerbate racial divides by making it harder for congregations to build relationships that bridge across racial groups. Because of their convenience and sense of solidarity, relationships among congregations that share the same racial composition tend to be more tight-knit or, in other words, tend to be in social circles where a friend of a friend is likely also to be a friend. When people build new friendships, they tend to choose friends of friends or people in some way already connected to their social group. They're "constrained by whom [they] already know." Congregations may experience this constraint as well. If most of a congregation's friends, friends of friends, and connections within its religious group and neighborhood share its racial group, it's going to be challenging to build relationships with congregations that have a different racial composition—even if the congregation greatly desires to do so.[9]

The lack of relationships between congregations that have different racial compositions reflects and contributes to racial divisions within central Alabama. A significant amount of research shows that friendships between social groups can lessen prejudice and antagonism, particularly when there are common interests and goals. One of the ways inter-group contact can reduce prejudice about another social group is through lessening negative emotions, like anxiety or threat, and boosting positive emotions, like empathy and trust. However, because many congregations tend to build relationships exclusively or primarily within their racial group, fewer congregations are taking advantage of opportunities to build the types of relationships that can reduce racial prejudice and division.[10]

RECAP AND NEXT STEPS

Relationships between racially similar congregations are very common. Barriers to building relationships with congregations that have different racial compositions include congregations' tendencies to build relationships within their religious groups, most of which are racially homogeneous; their tendencies to build relationships within their neighborhoods, many of which are racially segregated; and differences in theology, politics, and responses to the pandemic. Racially homogeneous relationships are quite convenient to develop and can provide meaningful support, especially for congregations of color, but they contribute to racial divisions in central Alabama.

In chapter 6, we turn to relationships between congregations that have differing racial compositions, which are not as common because they're, frankly, more difficult to develop and to sustain. However, these relationships have produced fruitful collaborations between congregations, especially when it comes to ministry in the community. I share practical insights from ministers about some dynamics that encourage healthy interracial relationships and other dynamics that can unintentionally undermine them.

QUESTIONS TO CONSIDER

1. How many of the congregations on your list have the same racial composition as your congregation?
2. How did you develop these relationships?
3. What support have you offered or received through them?
4. How much racial segregation is there in your community?
5. Has your congregation encountered barriers to building relationships with congregations that have different racial compositions? If so, which barriers?

Chapter 6

Partnering across Race

Many congregations desire to see faith communities play a central role in healing racial divisions but face challenges in doing so, particularly considering the ways in which religion has been used to justify slavery, racial segregation, and discrimination and to undercut racial justice efforts. For congregations that seek to lessen racial divisions, it's essential to build relationships with congregations from different racial groups because intergroup friendships are one of the most effective ways to learn about others' cultures and life experiences and to break down the stereotypes that contribute to prejudice and discrimination. Some congregations have done this to encourage racial reconciliation and to work together to pursue racial justice. They're, unfortunately, in the minority because of how racial divisions in central Alabama impact congregations' relationships.[1]

Due to strong tendencies to build relationships within one's own racial group and other barriers to partnerships across race, relationships between congregations with different racial compositions are not as common or convenient to develop. Just 30 percent of the relationships in figure 6.1 (236 of 793) bridge across racial groups. However, congregations' relationships across racial groups, when they're developed in healthy ways, can help to heal local racial divisions and can result in significant collaborations, many of which have strengthened congregations' ministries in the community. This chapter explores how congregations can build relationships with congregations that have a different racial composition, the types of support these relationships offer, how congregations can use these relationships to navigate opportunities and challenges, and practical tips about how to help these relationships to thrive and not undermine them.[2]

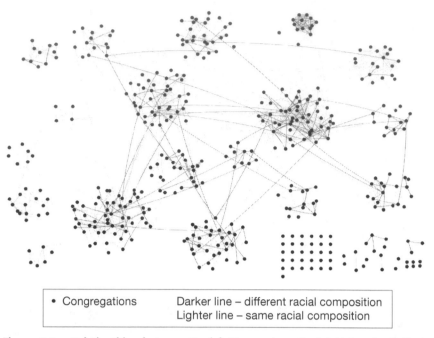

• Congregations	Darker line – different racial composition
	Lighter line – same racial composition

Figure 6.1.   Relationships between Racial Groups in a Social Network of Central Alabama Congregations. Created by the author using NodeXL Basic (http://nodexl. codeplex.com) from the Social Media Research Foundation (https://www.smrfounda-tion.org).

BUILDING RELATIONSHIPS
BETWEEN RACIAL GROUPS

Because of the religious, geographic, theological, and political barriers between congregations that have different racial compositions, congregations that seek to develop relationships between racial groups need to be thoughtful and purposeful about doing so. Here are four ways in which congregations can build relationships across racial groups.

1.   Some congregations have developed partnerships across race through programs that match congregations with the hope of promoting racial reconciliation. Here are two examples. A Presbyterian Church (U.S.A.) minister shared about Mission Reconcile,[3] a racial reconciliation ministry that paired his church with an African American Baptist church that had very different theological and political perspectives. Through this program, the churches were able to participate in workshops and to host joint worship services. In addition, a Jewish leader in Birmingham

mentioned a partnership with a predominantly African American congregation in a community west of Birmingham that developed through a specific program focused on extending hospitality between racial groups.

2. Other congregations have developed these partnerships through their ministerial associations, where clergy gather to learn from each other, to support each other, and to undertake joint projects.[4] An African American Baptist minister described how the local ministerial association in his community involves not only a wide range of denominations but also a significant number of white and African American ministers. A minister at a predominantly white, suburban Baptist congregation also shared about how his congregation is developing a partnership with a predominantly African American congregation because of a suggestion from its local Baptist association.

3. Some congregations have partnered together specifically to dialogue about race. An African American Baptist minister shared,

> A couple years ago we did a seminar where we got together [with a predominantly white nondenominational church], and we just talked about race. We went over to their church first and did race relations issues. The last one we did at our church was right after President Trump was elected because there were Black people that were really concerned about what he would bring into his administration, so we had a conversation with white churches, and we just talked about those issues.

4. Congregations can also build relationships with congregations from different racial groups through informal relationships between their ministers. An African American minister described the following get-together: "I just had breakfast with a Caucasian pastor friend yesterday, and we were talking about how we can show unity, especially in these times that we are in. With the rapid division that's taking place from all different aspects, how can we come together and show something different?" Another African American pastor shared how his relationships with white pastors have helped him to encourage other African American ministers to build interracial relationships: "Because some of my contemporaries [other ministers of color] have some negative thoughts concerning some of the [white] churches, having those relationships allows me to say, 'I know some [white] brothers who love the Lord and who I would trust with my life.'"

BENEFITS OF RELATIONSHIPS
BETWEEN RACIAL GROUPS

In my conversations with ministers whose congregations have relationships that bridge across racial groups, two types of benefits stood out.

Exchanging Ideas and Resources

Some white ministers shared about ideas and resources from African American congregations that have helped them to understand racial dynamics and to minister in a way that's less likely to reinforce racial divisions. One minister spoke about this extensively in our conversation.

> When I first got here, there's an older African American pastor who I sat down with, and he was like, "If you want to understand the history of why things are the way they are in our city, you need to read this book called *Some of My Best Friends Are Black* by Tanner Colby." He says, "If you drop down in Birmingham today and look around, you're probably going to be prejudiced. You're probably going to be a racist. You're going to see certain people prospering and other people in poverty, and you're going to make assumptions based upon those things. If you understand the history of how we got to where we are and why things are the way they are, hopefully, as a believer, instead of prejudice, you're going to have a lot of empathy in your heart."

This pastor also sees predominantly African American congregations as exemplars of faithful Christianity: "If we want to learn what it looks like to faithfully love our neighbors as ourselves while holding to the orthodoxy of Christian teaching, the historic Black Church is the example of that in the history of our country. In our own city, we have so much to learn about what it looks like to be a faithful Christian and church." These conversations have provided valuable resources that have helped this church to build partnerships across racial groups.

Here are two more examples of how predominantly white congregations have learned about ideas and resources from African American congregations, both of which involve Presbyterian Church (U.S.A.) congregations. One minister shared how, based on some conversations with African American leaders, "a group of us got together and started having [regular meetings about] what resources are there for a progressive white church trying not to stick its foot in its mouth, while being helpful and supportive." For another minister, a relationship with an African American colleague was particularly helpful for navigating a conversation around race within her congregation.

One day after worship, I had someone offer a critique that there were too many uses of dark versus light in the liturgy that cast darkness as a bad thing, which I hadn't seen that way. We often talk about dark and light and that light will shine through darkness and the darkness cannot overcome it, but a concern that that equates darkness with being bad is not a direction we want to go. So [my African American colleague is] one of those people I can call up and say, "Can you talk with me about this from your perspective as a person of color, help me with this, and can you give me some good books to read?"

Through these relationships, these pastors have been able to access a wider range of viewpoints and resources in order to minister in ways that more intentionally affirm racial diversity.[5]

Collaborations

Partnerships between congregations that have different racial compositions have also produced fruitful collaborations. I will present a variety of collaborations in the next section, so I'll just describe one here. A minister at a predominantly white suburban congregation shared about a racial justice collaboration that took place in 2020. Following the death of George Floyd, there were mostly peaceful protests for racial justice in Birmingham during the summer of 2020. However, there were some more violent incidents near a Confederate monument in a downtown park. Alabama law prohibits the removal of historical monuments and penalizes removal with a fine. This minister explained, "A group of us got together after the murder of George Floyd, really a broad spectrum of faith leaders partnered to help raise the money required to pay the fine for the Confederate Memorial in the park." Many community leaders praised the removal of this monument as a step toward healing racial divisions in the Birmingham metro area.[6] This collaboration would not have been possible without relationships between congregations from different racial groups. This minister described the following: "Being led by some of our historically Black congregations, some of the predominantly white congregations were thinking through how we can support and assist in a way that's not domineering. I'm especially grateful for our local partners who see things outside of our perspective." This example illustrates how collaborations that draw on a wider variety of perspectives and resources are often more effective.[7]

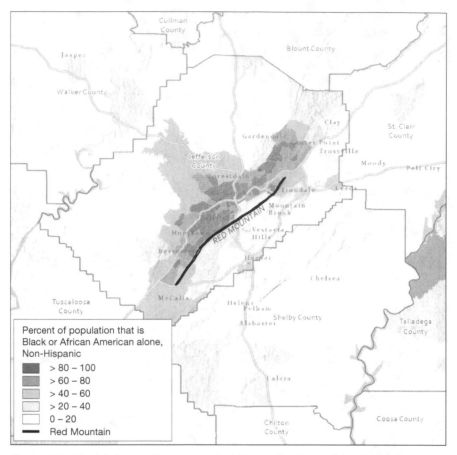

Figure 6.2. Racial Segregation across Red Mountain. Created by the author using ArcGIS with assistance from Jonathan Fleming.

NAVIGATING OPPORTUNITIES AND CHALLENGES
TOGETHER ACROSS RACIAL GROUPS

There are a variety of ways in which congregations can draw on relationships across racial groups to navigate opportunities and challenges, and I share some of these stories from Birmingham and Tuscaloosa, the home of the University of Alabama, below. Before we turn to them, though, I'd like to introduce a bit of local lingo. Some of the ministers in the Birmingham metro area, in discussing partnerships across race, use the phrase "over the mountain." This is a reference to Red Mountain, a key physical landmark that is depicted in figure 6.2. Red Mountain gets its name from its iron ore, which fueled Birmingham's steel industry, and its impact goes far beyond the steel industry. Red Mountain represents a significant line of segregation, in which communities just north of Red Mountain tend to be predominantly African American and communities south of Red Mountain tend to be predominantly white.[8] Many partnerships across race in the Birmingham metro area involve congregations on different sides of Red Mountain.

An African American Baptist Church in Birmingham

This church emphasizes evangelism, teaching and discipling attenders, building relationships through fellowship, and worship. According to its minister, "Evangelism is the process of outreach, discipleship is the teaching ministry of the church and equipping people for service, fellowship is the caring of the body [of Christ, or the congregation], and worship is the premium on God in weekend services." This congregation is in a lower-income neighborhood, and it has a significant emphasis on ministering to its surrounding community. Its opportunities and challenges are mainly related to its community ministries. This minister described how this played out:

> The great opportunity was, during this pandemic, we remained faithful during that time, although public worship was semi-suspended—I say "semi" because we reduced the number of people that we allowed to attend public worship—to comply with the CDC guidelines, but we were able to service the community more with food boxes. Each week, we distributed more than 1,500 food boxes to people within the community, the entire time from March [2020] all the way [to the point of the interview in 2021].

In addition, this minister shared how this church was able to expand its financial resources and to make progress on a building project during the pandemic. "This is a blessing because we were able to begin the construction during the pandemic. When most churches were closed, we were able to experience financial growth, so now the challenge is that we're working on community revitalization to bring the community alive around the church."

This church's minister described how his church builds relationships with predominantly white and predominantly African American congregations in order to bring spiritual healing and revival to the area.

> We have encouraged intentional formations with other Black and white congregations, so we've tried to be intentional about encouraging those kinds of relationships to foster the Kingdom. We believe that a little light in darkness becomes a great light, and we believe that there are a lot of Christians throughout the entire area and a lot of people that have been praying for a long time for real revival to take place within the inner city. Jefferson County [where Birmingham is located] is perhaps one of the most fragmented communities in

all of the Deep South, and we believe that the way to begin to impact it most is through the church, and several like-minded pastors have convened around that kind of thing.

These relationships have also fostered collaborations that have helped this congregation to minister in its community.

This church's minister shared how collaborations have strengthened its food and housing ministries. During the pandemic, the minister explained, "We invited [over twenty] other churches to come to our church to pick up food items that they could then distribute in their own churches, so it was more of a community effort that included Black and white congregations coming together." This church sees partnerships with "over the mountain" congregations as essential for effective ministry in its community.

> One of the principles of community revitalization is redistribution. The challenge of the inner city is developing appropriate housing, and in the larger white congregations, there are persons who are builders and persons who own businesses, and they're looking, in a real sense, to make an impact in the inner city. Building those relationships can lead to effective partnerships that can impact what's going on in the inner city. It's really a question of continuing to open the door and help people to understand that the opportunity does exist and that it's truly a Kingdom opportunity. Many large white congregations send missionaries across the world. We believe there's a mission field in the inner city, and so while we're sending people across the world, let's send people across the mountain as well and engage in some of the meaningful activities that are going on there, coming alongside churches.

According to this minister, these collaborations are valuable "because we can do more together than we can separately, and there are gifts and abilities that may not necessarily be singularly located within our congregation." Through these collaborations, this congregation has increased its capacity and resources to respond to opportunities and challenges in its community.

A Recently Founded Church in Birmingham

This church has a strong orientation toward evangelism and making disciples, and it intentionally seeks to contextualize this mission in its immediate neighborhood. A pastor described the following:

> We're not just Christians or a church in a vacuum but in a particular place, so what ways do we desire to see the Gospel come to bear in the city where the Lord's called us? Just knowing Birmingham's history of the lines of division that were created in our city's inception and, in some ways, only got stronger at

integration with how our city's laid out, we're trying to learn how to minister across these different lines of division, culturally and economically.

This congregation stands out for its newness and youth; it was founded within the past ten years, and over 80 percent of its attenders are between the ages of eighteen and thirty.

Some of this congregation's opportunities and challenges are related to bridging across these divisions. Here's what its pastor shared about the theological and political divisions it is seeking to bridge.

> A lot of churches put a lot of emphasis on Great Commission and reaching the nations [i.e., evangelism], which is great, but often those people neglect their neighborhood. And then there are other people that are really great at ministering to people in their neighborhood but don't have a vision beyond that. We want to see the Great Commission [evangelism] and the Great Commandment [serving others] go together. . . . We are a blue area in a very red state, and the last eighteen months has revealed a lot of that—from George Floyd and the pandemic to all kinds of things. There are some differences in how different groups approach the same issue, and so I've seen over [recent] years more polarization culturally and politically, so I think that Christians who maybe would have been celebrating what we were trying to do [in the early 2010s] may be more suspicious of that now, with suspicion toward conversations about critical race theory and all kinds of things. I try to disciple our people to, instead of being discipled by your favorite news media outlet, let's see what the Scriptures say about these things.

In seeking to build bridges, this church has developed partnerships with both white and African American congregations from both sides of Red Mountain.

Here's an example of how this church is partnering with a predominantly African American church to address divisions within the church and community. The pastor explained,

> There's an event called the (&) Campaign,[9] and a book called *Compassion (&) Conviction* that's written for folks who feel more politically homeless right now. How can we be Christians that hold to certain convictions that Christians have held to through the centuries, while also showing compassion in these things? So that's what the "&" stands for, for biblical values and social justice. It's an event where we're trying to bring more like-minded Christians together in our city that care about a lot of these things, while also wanting to hold firmly to Christian convictions.

This church intentionally nurtures relationships with churches from different racial groups in order to recruit partners that are also seeking to bridge across these differences.

A Southern Baptist Church and a National Baptist Church in Tuscaloosa

There is a wonderful relationship between a predominantly white Southern Baptist church and a predominantly African American National Baptist church in Tuscaloosa, and I am grateful to have talked with ministers from both churches about it. First, I introduce both churches and the opportunities and challenges that they are facing, and then I describe their relationship and collaborations.

According to one of its pastors, the Southern Baptist church values missions and evangelism. "Our mission is based on the Great Commission to go therefore and make disciples." Through its worship, small groups, and service in the community, it hopes to help people to grow spiritually. This church is also engaged in missions within the United States and internationally, although COVID-19 has prevented mission trips. It has numerous mission partners through the Southern Baptist International Mission Board, North American Mission Board, and the Alabama Baptist State Board of Missions. The pandemic has impacted this congregation's worship, small groups, and financial giving. This pastor described the resulting dynamic: "When we came back from not meeting at all, initially we went to three worship services, but the [Sunday afternoon] service did not work well. So we went back to just the two worship services, and with the number of people that have actually returned, we're able to accommodate them in two worship services." In addition, "the [earlier] service is very traditional. Before vaccination, it was very low attended, but then as the senior adults and some of the others got vaccinated, attendance kind of went back to 60 percent, maybe 70 percent" in both services. At the point of the interview, this church's small groups were still meeting virtually. Although the pandemic did not have much of an impact on this church's finances, this church did rethink how people can give financially, including through online giving and mailing checks rather than bringing a financial gift to an in-person gathering. This pastor shared how this church has actually "seen an uptick in missional giving this year, so that's been a good thing."

The National Baptist church, according to its pastor, has the following dynamic: "[It's] very progressive not only in our theology but in our methodology of doing ministry. We are justice-driven. We are very engaged in the community. We participate in a lot of outreach in our community—food drives, Christmas events, and protest rallies." In addition, the pastor added, "We've also been involved in blocking liquor stores from entering the community because [the church] is in an urban context, is in a predominantly African American, high-poverty area of Tuscaloosa." This church has experienced opportunities to serve in its community and to expand its reach using technology, as well as challenges with generating financial and human resources. Its pastor described, "When you are doing ministry in an urban context, there's always a need. When we have our food drives, we've never left with food, so we always feed [hundreds of] families each time." This church is also taking advantage of opportunities to reach out in its community using technology "because, in COVID, that's probably going to be the primary source of disseminating and communicating the Gospel." According to its pastor, key challenges involve resources. "To do the type of ministry we feel called to do, it requires resources. We have a nonprofit, a 501(c)(3) association, and we've gotten a few grants, but probably the biggest challenge is having the resources, both financial and human, to do what you are called to do in the community."

The relationship between these churches has nurtured some rich collaborations. Here's how the Southern Baptist minister described the collaborations.

> We partner very strongly with an African American church on the west side to where we provide financial support, we provide tutors for their after-school program, and we have provided workers for their Vacation Bible School. We have invited them, and they've have gone along with us on national mission trips to where they would not have been able to go and serve in that manner without the partnership being there.

And here is how the National Baptist minister described them.

> I have to mention [the Southern Baptist Church] because [that church] has a lot of financial resources, but we brought things to the table that [the SBC church] didn't have. In some of our mission trips, our congregation led the worship. We went to housing projects, and we did praise and worship and dance. [The SBC church] put up the bill in terms of a lot of the food and transportation, but [our church] took a leading role in the worship arts and things like that.

In addition, the National Baptist minister shared,

> There's a great need in west Tuscaloosa for tutorial services after school, not only due to the achievement gaps, but due to the fact that a lot of parents in urban communities are single parents, and they work. We know that children left alone are not always engaged in productive activities. They're very seldom learning. So what [our church] did in partnerships with our nonprofit is to create an after school program and a summer program, which we do in our facility. It's our program, but [the SBC church] supplies the majority of the tutors through their college ministry. The more frequent and consistent the collaborations are, the more trust is built. That's an everyday, every week collaboration, so a lot of trust is built there.

Through these collaborations, these churches have been able to pool resources so that they can respond more effectively to opportunities to minister in their community.

IT'S NOT ALWAYS EASY

The main downside of partnerships across racial groups is that, because of the barriers between racial groups, it can be very challenging for the ministers and congregations who are seeking to build these bridges. Sometimes it can be difficult to find congregations that are willing to engage in dialogue. An African American minister shared,

> Black pastors are saying, "Well, we're not going to have those conversations as long as white pastors are not willing to say that Black Lives Matter too, so we're not having more conversations about reconciliation." I'm saying to Black pastors, "Listen, someone has to continue to keep conversations going. If all white and Black pastors say that we're not having the conversations any longer, then we as the Church of Jesus Christ will continue to be divided."

Ministers who are developing these partnerships can also experience resistance from white congregations and congregations of color. This minister described his experience.

> There's a price to pay for being a bridge. Being educated at [a predominantly white seminary] created this tension within my current context with other African American pastors [who are] saying, "Why are you going to get educated over in the white community? You're going to be preaching to African American people." Sometimes people from the white side have made it clear that, really, "you don't belong here because you don't have the IQ to be in this space," and then from the Black side it's that, "how dare you explain to us how white people and white pastors are processing things." Being that bridge, sometimes I've only gotten pushback.

Because of the barriers between racial groups, it's not always easy to build these partnerships. If you'd like to do so, please know that you need to be intentional about and committed to it.

TIPS FOR YOUR CONGREGATION

There are approaches that nurture healthy relationships across race, and others that are more likely to undermine them. To start, it's important to avoid the "white savior complex," which assumes that white people ought to fix or save "broken" people and communities of color.[10] Some ministers from predominantly white congregations, in seeking to avoid this complex, have focused on building partnerships with congregations of color to support the ministry that they're doing. Here's what a suburban Presbyterian Church in America minister shared: "Our desire is not just to catapult or parachute people over the mountain into the urban areas of Birmingham but build relationships with churches inside the city. We utilize [a faith-based, nonprofit community development organization] to help with that. They have such a strong tie with urban churches." This congregation is careful in its ministry over the mountain because, as the minister said, "We don't want to look like we're the great white hope. That's why we want to work with [congregations of color in Birmingham]. If we can use our resources to undergird and support them, that's what we want to be about." It's detrimental when white congregations fail to do this. An African American minister shared,

A local white congregation was going into a neighborhood that was majority Black. Why is it that you think that these people here are so lost or so much in need of Jesus? You never asked us what we were doing in the community. Sometimes it's an insult to assume, especially in that sphere, that they [white churches] have the Gospel, and "if you don't do it how we do, then we have to fix what you've done wrong."

If you're a white congregation that is seeking to build interracial partnerships, come alongside to support, and do not disregard the ministry of congregations of color.

It's also important for predominantly white congregations to understand the complexity of racial divisions because it can help them not to undermine congregations of color unintentionally. A suburban Cooperative Baptist minister described how "people of faith must not turn a cold shoulder; blind eye; deaf ear; closed fist; or, even worse, closed heart to people who are marginalized and dispossessed. The systemic nature of some of these challenges and any commitment to redress those inequities require long-term commitments. There's no quick fix in any of them." This congregation is careful, in its ministry in communities of color, to primarily work through partnerships with congregations of color and other urban ministries and not to circumvent their role within their community. The pastor explained what happened in some of the neighborhoods of color where this congregation has partnerships:

People are highly sensitive about predominantly white congregations coming in. Some predominantly white churches' efforts have not been as well received because the perception of some of the African American churches is that they were bypassed, and we have been careful not to do that. We've also worked

with individuals in those areas that have come to our attention again through
relationships that members of our church have had with individuals in those
communities. When someone has a need, we try not only to meet that need, but
we try to connect that individual with congregations [in their community] that
might be able to provide longer-term support.

White congregations that seek to nurture partnerships across race must be
aware of how interwoven racial divisions are in our society and be careful not
to bypass congregations of color.

Because of the racial divisions among congregations, congregations that
effectively build partnerships across race also know that it takes time to build
trust. A minister of the recently founded church in Birmingham, which I profiled earlier in this chapter, described how his church was founded.

There was a lot of suspicion—understandably so—from pastors that were pas-
toring historic Black congregations in our city because of the history of our city
and people who claim to be Christians, who look like me, blowing up buildings
and houses. There've also been some other [white] congregations who have not
built as many relationships [with African American congregations] but have
gotten a lot of people that have come out of historic Black churches into their
churches and have maybe, [some African American pastors] felt like, stolen
their sheep. We've seen this within ministry in our city where people come in
for a little while and then leave. I think time tests all kinds of desires.

To build healthy partnerships across race, know that it takes time to develop
trust. Be patient and willing to do what it takes.

A key factor that can undermine partnerships across race involves congregations and ministers of color not being represented equally in joint events
or ministerial gatherings. An African American minister shared, "There
was a city-wide revival hosted by one of the [white] local Southern Baptist
churches. They invited us to come, and they were like, 'This is for the city.'
But there was nothing about our city that was represented in the preaching,
in the worship songs, in the participants. Is this for the city, or is this for
you?" In addition, this minister shared his experience in his local ministerial
association: "Eighty percent of the white clergy are full-time, and 80 percent,
if not 90 percent, of the Black clergy are bivocational [working another job
in addition to being a minister]. There has to be a constant reminder to my
full-time pastor friends that that's not—how am I supposed to get to meetings
on Tuesdays at 11:15 a.m. and then get back to work?" If you'd like to build
partnerships across race through joint events or ministerial groups, make sure
that ministers and congregations from different racial groups can equally participate and that their cultures and styles are equally represented.

Lastly, effective partnerships across race involve reciprocal and mutual engagement from congregations of different racial compositions. A suburban Cooperative Baptist minister emphasized mutuality in describing a new partnership with a predominantly African American congregation. "We are now having conversations about how we proceed in respectful and in mutually beneficial ways, not paternalistic or condescending. If you approach these relationships from a mutually beneficial standpoint, you recognize that each of these partners has as much to offer us as we have to offer them." However, some ministers of color have experienced situations where opportunities were not reciprocated.[11] An African American minister, in seeking to build partnerships across race, expressed to white ministers,

> If you want your people to better understand the experience of their neighbors in this community, you need to have Black preachers come to your pulpit. In me coming, I'm not coming as entertainment. I have to be presented as just as serious of a preacher as a white man standing and preaching. It's always funny when the invitations [for white ministers] to come to the Black congregations are numerous, but the invitations for it to be reciprocated [for Black ministers to preach at white churches] are very limited. So Black congregations are having to model what it is that dignity should look like, even to those who are better resourced and in the dominant, majority culture.

In cross-racial partnerships, it's crucial that congregations and ministers of color are treated as equal partners in ministry.

Here's a summary of these tips:

- Avoid the "white savior complex."
- Understand the complexity of racial divisions.
- Take time to build trust.
- Make sure that ministers and congregations from different racial groups can equally participate and that their cultures and styles are equally represented.
- Nurture reciprocal and mutual engagement from congregations of different racial compositions.

RECAP AND WHAT'S NEXT

Congregations that seek to address racial divisions within their communities cannot do so without partnerships with congregations that have different racial compositions, but these partnerships are not as common or easy for congregations to develop. Interracial partnerships can help congregations to navigate opportunities and challenges through expanding the range of ideas and resources and the opportunities for collaboration that are available to them. These partnerships can thrive when congregations from different racial groups come alongside each other to support each other's ministries and allow each other to equally contribute to the partnership, but there can be quite negative consequences when these things don't happen.

In chapter 7, I conclude the book with practical next steps for your congregation. I offer advice about how to build relationships with other congregations through friendships between ministers, joint events, gatherings of ministers, and pulpit exchanges. I also summarize insights from the book about the advantages and disadvantages of different relationships. My goal is to help you to identify the relationship types you're interested in developing and strengthening so that you can respond to the particular opportunities and challenges that your congregation is facing.

QUESTIONS TO CONSIDER

1. How many of the congregations on your list have a different racial composition?
2. How did you develop these relationships?
3. What support have you offered or received through them?
4. How can you use insights from this chapter to create and strengthen relationships with congregations that have a different racial composition?
5. How might these relationships help your congregation to navigate its opportunities and challenges and to support other congregations?

Chapter 7

Practical Next Steps

In this final chapter, I'd like to offer some practical advice about how to build relationships with other congregations to find the support you need to navigate the opportunities and challenges you're experiencing.

FOUR WAYS TO BUILD RELATIONSHIPS

There are numerous ways to build relationships between congregations, and I'd like to give you advice on four: friendships between ministers, joint events, ministerial groups, and pulpit exchanges. These are the four about which I surveyed ministers and leaders and that I've used to create the network images of relationships that I've shared throughout the book.[1]

Friendships between Ministers

A very common type of relationship between congregations involves friendships between their ministers. Ninety percent of the relationships in figure 7.1 (714 of 793) involve a friendship between ministers, and they're so common that you'd have to look fairly closely at figure 7.1 to find relationships that don't involve friendships between ministers. We've already talked in this book about how many ministers have too much to do and not enough time to do it,[2] and friendships with ministers from other congregations might be the easiest way to start building these relationships since they don't have to involve collaborating for an event, joining a ministerial group, or committing to preach at each other's congregations.

These friendships have significant benefits both for ministers and congregations, and I'd like to remind you of some content (and some quotes) from chapter 1. A significant number of congregational ministers and leaders are experiencing difficulties with physical and mental health, stress, and burnout,

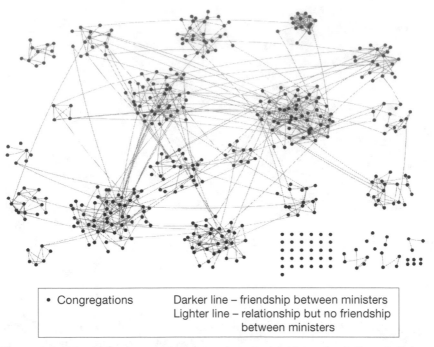

Figure 7.1. Friendships between Ministers in a Social Network of Central Alabama Congregations. Created by the author using NodeXL Basic (http://nodexl.codeplex.com) from the Social Media Research Foundation (https://www.smrfoundation.org).

and supportive relationships, especially with other ministers, can nurture their health and help them to cope with the stress and challenges of ministry.

> We found that pastors with flourishing mental health were more likely to have strong relationships than pastors with low mental health. Clergy are surrounded by people. However, we shouldn't confuse social interaction with supportive relationships. Clergy may interact with people all day, and they may frequently provide support to others, but that doesn't mean they're receiving support from others. . . . What are sources of emotional support for pastors? The most frequently mentioned sources were spouses, friends, and clergy colleagues.[3]

These relationships are beneficial not just for health but also for leading congregations well.

> In many conversations with pastors and denominational leaders . . . , clergy friendships emerged as of considerable importance for sustaining ministry in challenging times. Having close friends is in itself not a guarantee of excellent pastoral leadership; however, without the support, companionship, mutual critique, and joy that friends offer, without those with whom one can be vulnerable

and share deeply, it is difficult, if not impossible, to sustain . . . [an] excellent ministry.[4]

In this network, friendships between ministers are the most common way congregations build relationships with each other, and I hope that, if you're a congregational minister or leader, you can build them and find support through them.[5]

If you're a congregational minister or leader, here are some practical tips for building relationships with other ministers and leaders. First, many friendships are built around a commonality. Think about what you'd like this to be. It could be the same religious group, the same racial group, the same local community, a similar preaching or worship style, a certain perspective about scripture or theology, a commitment to a particular type of or approach to ministry, or other things. Then reach out to another minister or leader. Maybe you have a mutual friend who can introduce you. Try to build the relationship through conversations, getting together for coffee or a meal, and interacting regularly enough to build trust. As your relationship grows, pray together, share about what's going on in your ministry and personal life, and explore and learn about something together that you both care about (this could be related to ministry, hobbies, or other things). This foundation will help you to support each other through the joys and challenges of ministry.

Joint Events

Many congregations work together and pool resources to organize and host joint events, and about 75 percent of the relationships in figure 7.2 (599 of 793) involve at least one joint event. In my conversations with ministers and leaders, they mentioned a wide range of events, including religious services, talks and lectures, retreats, conferences, social gatherings, summer camps, children's and youth ministry programming, social advocacy events, and community service activities.

The main benefit of these joint events is that they allow congregations to pool resources and to do more than they could do alone. Most congregations are small in size and don't have the staff, volunteers, financial resources, and space to do everything that they'd like. Congregations can often do more when they pool resources. Perhaps one congregation has the space to host an after-school tutoring program for a nearby elementary school, and another congregation recruits the volunteer tutors. For a joint religious service, one congregation can host the event, another can supply the teacher or preacher, and a third can provide the musicians. Congregations with small numbers of children and youth can also work together to have joint gatherings and community service opportunities so that their children and youth can build

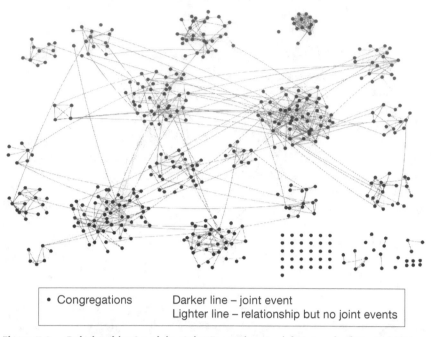

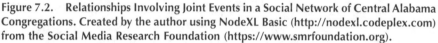

Figure 7.2.   Relationships Involving Joint Events in a Social Network of Central Alabama Congregations. Created by the author using NodeXL Basic (http://nodexl.codeplex.com) from the Social Media Research Foundation (https://www.smrfoundation.org).

relationships with a wider range of peers. Multiple congregations can pool financial resources to bring in a speaker, whom none alone would have been able to afford, for a retreat or conference. These examples illustrate how joint events can expand congregations' opportunities for ministry.[6]

If you're a minister or leader and you'd like to develop more joint events, here's some practical advice. To start, talk with congregations where you have friendships to see if they're interested in partnering or if they can suggest a congregation with whom to partner. A denominational leader or local community organization may also be able to recommend a partner. In choosing a partner, be open about your values, the joint event you're interested in, and what you hope will come about because of the joint event. Think carefully about your congregation's resources and what you need a partner to contribute for the joint event to be effective, and focus on developing a partnership with a congregation whose resources can complement yours. After you've developed a partnership, be willing to nurture it over time and to maintain communication about collaborations and how things are going. Allow each congregation to contribute as meaningfully and substantively as their resources allow. Be clear about who is doing and contributing specific things so that everyone knows what's expected.[7]

Ministerial Groups

Congregations can also build relationships when their ministers and leaders participate in the same ministerial group, and in about 60 percent of the relationships in figure 7.3 (491 of 793), ministers from both congregations are involved in the same ministerial group. Ministerial groups are settings where ministers gather to build relationships, pray, encourage each other, share ideas and resources, develop collaborations, and do other things. There are a variety of types of groups that ministers and leaders can join, and I'll introduce three types here. Some ministerial groups take place through gatherings organized by local Baptist associations, regional Presbyterian presbyteries, Methodist districts, Catholic and Episcopal dioceses, nondenominational networks, and other religious groups. Other ministerial associations are focused around a local community and include ministers and leaders from a variety of religious

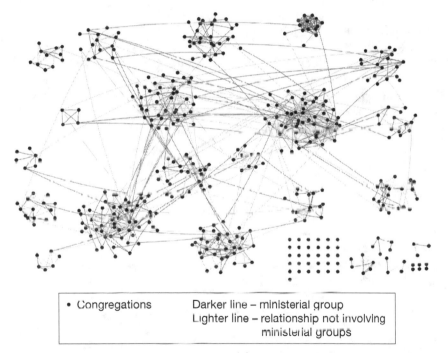

- Congregations   Darker line – ministerial group
Lighter line – relationship not involving
ministerial groups

Figure 7.3. Relationships Involving Ministerial Groups in a Social Network of Central Alabama Congregations. Created by the author using NodeXL Basic (http://nodexl. codeplex.com) from the Social Media Research Foundation (https://www.smrfoundation.org).

groups and/or racial groups. Ministers and leaders can also gather in clergy peer groups, which tend to be smaller and less formal. These groups provide ministers and leaders with opportunities to learn together, support each other, and offer accountability to each other, and they allow ministers and leaders to have more autonomy in shaping the identity and goals of the group. Some clergy peer groups are supported by parachurch organizations that provide resources for congregational ministers and leaders, and other clergy peer groups are developed informally among ministers.[8]

Relationships within ministerial groups have many of the benefits for clergy health that I mentioned when discussing friendships between ministers, so I am going to focus on other benefits here. These gatherings provide important venues for ministers and leaders to learn about ideas and resources that they can then use in their congregations, and to share ideas and resources that have been helpful in their ministry. In addition, these gatherings have practical impacts within congregations. Congregations whose ministers and leaders participate in these gatherings tend to have a wider range of attenders, including teenagers and newly attending adults, who are involved in ministries, leadership roles, and decision making at the congregation, and they tend to have a stronger emphasis on ministering and advocating in their community.[9] If you're a minister or leader who's involved in a ministerial gathering, I hope that you are experiencing some of these benefits.

Here are some tips about building relationships through ministerial groups. First, look around to see what ministerial groups are available in your religious group or local community. Reach out to other ministers you already know to see what opportunities they're aware of. If there are options available, visit some of the gatherings to see if one may be a good fit for you. Some communities also have parachurch organizations that provide resources for ministers and congregations. If you know of organizations like this in your community, see if they organize gatherings of clergy or have any suggestions for already-established gatherings. If there are not opportunities to join gatherings within your religious group or local community, reach out to friends who are ministers and leaders to see if they're interested in developing an informal group. In these groups, how much you benefit is dependent on how much all members can invest, and it can be helpful to set standards for how much ministers are expected to engage in order to create a more enriching and supportive experience.[10]

Pulpit Exchanges

A final way to build relationships involves pulpit exchanges, where a minister from one congregation teaches or preaches at another congregation. Sometime this is just one way, where one minister speaks at another congregation but it's

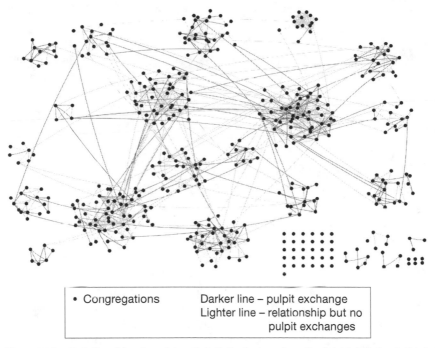

• Congregations	Darker line – pulpit exchange
	Lighter line – relationship but no
	pulpit exchanges

Figure 7.4. **Relationships Involving Pulpit Exchanges in a Social Network of Central Alabama Congregations. Created by the author using NodeXL Basic (http://nodexl. codeplex.com) from the Social Media Research Foundation (https://www.smrfounda-tion.org).**

not reciprocated. Other times, the exchange goes both ways, where ministers swap pulpits either on the same day or on different days. Pulpit exchanges are not as common, and about 40 percent of the relationships in figure 7.4 (325 of 793) involve pulpit exchanges. These exchanges are beneficial in providing ministers with opportunities to speak to a wider range of people and in allowing attenders to hear a wider variety of preaching and teaching styles, ideas, and perspectives.[11]

If you're a minister and you'd like to develop a pulpit exchange, start with congregations with whom you already have a connection through a friendship with another minister, a collaboration, or a ministerial group. For some ministers and leaders, it can take a lot of trust to let another person speak to their congregation, and it's often easiest to do pulpit exchanges when there's already an established relationship. Think carefully about the range of perspectives and cultures to which you're willing to expose your attenders. Some ministers might want to limit pulpit exchanges to other ministers within their religious group that have similar theological views, while other ministers may be open to engaging with a wider range of theological perspectives and racial and ethnic cultures. If it's possible, make sure that the pulpit exchange is mutual, where both ministers get the opportunity to teach or preach at each other's congregation. This creates a stronger relationship between the congregations and signals that both congregations' cultures, perspectives, and contributions are valuable.

TIES BETWEEN CONGREGATIONS OR
TIES BETWEEN MINISTERS?

Throughout this project, I've had some people ask me if I'm really just studying relationships between ministers (and not actually relationships between congregations) because some of the ways congregations can build relationships, like friendships between ministers and ministerial groups, are more minister-focused. It is the case that the relationships between congregations that I've studied are more oriented around their ministers. For example, you'll notice that I haven't talked about friendships between attenders at different congregations, which is *definitely* a way that congregations can build relationships. It was much easier to interview one person at each congregation to learn about the congregation's connections, and it would have been much more challenging and time intensive to ask all of the attenders at each of the congregations about the other congregations where they have friends. (I would have had to keep track of tens of thousands of attenders. "So-and-so is my friend, but I don't know what congregation they attend. Can you figure it out?" I don't have a list of attenders at each congregation, and many ministers would not have been comfortable sharing one with me. Can you imagine?) I'll acknowledge that I'm not capturing all possible relationships between congregations and that some relationships between congregations might be stronger than others, depending on whether the relationship only involves the ministers or involves both ministers and attenders.

However, I'm not willing to say that this study isn't about relationships between congregations, even when some congregations are only connected through a friendship between their ministers, and here's why. If, through a friendship with another minister or a ministerial group, a minister receives support that nurtures his or her well-being and effectiveness in ministry, that can make a meaningful impact in his or her congregation. In addition, ministers can share ideas and resources which were developed by leaders and attenders within their congregation with other congregations through friendships with their ministers or ministerial groups. In this way, attenders in one congregation can provide meaningful resources for attenders in another congregation, even if the attenders don't know each other.[12]

SUPPORT ACROSS DIFFERENT RELATIONSHIP TYPES

Next, I'd like to review the relationship types I presented in chapters 2–6, the kinds of support that they do (or do not) provide, and advice about how to develop them.

Relationships within religious groups, the topic of chapter 2, are quite convenient to develop, and it's often easier to trust other congregations that have similar approaches to theology and ministry. Benefits include strong friendships, emotional support, the exchange of trusted ideas and resources, and convenient opportunities to develop collaborations. However, relationships within religious groups can limit the range of ideas, resources, and opportunities for collaborations that are available to congregations, and they can also (often unintentionally) increase competition between congregations for attenders. It's easiest for congregations to develop these relationships through religious group and denominational gatherings, and nondenominational congregations can do so through a growing number of nondenominational networks.

Tight-knit relationships within distinctive religious groups, which I profiled among Churches of Christ and Latter-day Saints wards in chapter 3, can produce even richer support for congregations, including close and trusting relationships, frequent opportunities to brainstorm and to exchange trusted resources, and an even easier time developing collaborations. These tight-knit relationships can, however, constrain congregations from innovating or even from deviating in minor ways from other congregations within their religious group, and they can make it more difficult for congregations to build relationships outside of their religious group. The same advice about how to develop relationships within religious groups applies here.

Relationships between religious groups, which I explored in chapter 4, are not as common or convenient for congregations to develop. Theologically conservative congregations tend to connect with congregations from other conservative religious groups, while liberal churches and some non-Christian congregations tend to bridge across wider theological differences to encourage religious tolerance and to work toward social justice. Relationships between religious groups tend to provide congregations with wider ranges of ideas, resources, and opportunities for collaboration, but they don't tend to be as close as relationships within religious groups. Congregations can develop these relationships through, for example, interfaith ministerial associations and informal friendships.

There are numerous barriers between congregations that have different racial compositions, the topic of chapter 5, which include congregations' tendencies to build relationships within racially homogeneous religious groups or racially segregated neighborhoods, as well as theological and political differences. These barriers make it quite convenient for congregations to develop relationships within their racial group and quite challenging to build bridges across racial groups. Congregations of color, in particular, can benefit from racially homogeneous relationships through creating a safe space where they find support and solidarity without racial prejudice and discrimination. However, the racial barriers between congregations reflect and reinforce racial divisions in central Alabama.

Relationships between congregations with different racial compositions, the focus of chapter 6, are not as common due to the barriers discussed in chapter 5. Key benefits include access to a wider range of ideas and resources and some very fruitful collaborations. Congregations can build these partnerships through racial reconciliation programs, ministerial associations, dialogues, and informal friendships, but they're not always easy to develop. Congregations that wish to do so need to be sensitive to racial and cultural differences, supportive of other ministers and congregations, interested in building trust over a long period of time, and committed to providing equitable ways for congregations with different racial compositions to contribute.

CONCLUDING THOUGHTS

I'd like to conclude with a few final pieces of advice.

Do What You Can

In multiple chapters of this book, I've mentioned how much ministers have to do and how many ministers work over forty hours a week. Because of this, it's important for ministers to do what they can in what relationships they build. I want to help you to find support and resources through relationships with the congregations around you, but I don't want this book just to be one more thing you don't have time to do. As you build relationships, do what's manageable. If that means only relationships within your religious group where you're already getting together with other ministers at different gatherings and events, only relationships through a local ministerial association, or just the ministers you're already close friends with, do what works and what isn't overburdensome for you.

Nurture Close Friendships

Close friendships are likely where you're going to find the richest support, so please do your best to nurture these friendships. These relationships tend to be stronger, more trusting, more emotionally warm, and more likely to be based on a similarity. They tend to involve more time spent together and to be more reciprocal, where support is mutually offered and received. We're more likely to take advantage of ideas, resources, and opportunities offered by our friends because of the trust within the relationship. Close friendships are also very important in ministry because ministers and leaders are more likely to be on the giving end of support than on the receiving end. Close friendships with other ministers and leaders, who understand the joys and challenges of congregational ministry and leadership, can be valuable sources of support. We all need people in our lives who will be there for us no matter what, and close friends are more likely to do this for us.[13]

Don't Forget about Acquaintances

Having said this, please don't overlook your acquaintances. They may not be the most consistent or strongest sources of support in our lives, but they're valuable because they connect us to diverse groups and to a wider range of social circles. We often hear about new ideas or opportunities from acquaintances before we hear about them from friends. When I was considering applying to Samford, a short interaction with a Samford graduate at a conference helped me to feel like Samford would be a good fit for me, and this was important because none of my family members or close friends had any connection with Samford. Keeping up with acquaintances may help you to learn about a helpful new resource for congregational ministry or a wider range of opportunities to serve in the community. Collaborations with partners who are different from us—and who are more likely to be acquaintances—also tend to be more effective because they draw on a wider range of perspectives and resources. As you build partnerships across differences, please review the practical tips in chapter 6 about approaching differences with kindness, compassion, respect, and equity, not judgment or prejudice.[14]

THANK YOU!

Thanks for reading this book! I hope that you've been able to get some practical guidance about relationships you can build and strengthen as you navigate the opportunities and challenges that your congregation is experiencing. The congregations around you can be some of your greatest sources of support. If you've found this book helpful, please let other congregations, ministers, and leaders know about it. If we all care for each other through offering emotional support, ideas, resources, and opportunities for collaboration, we will be better equipped to navigate current and future changes, challenges, and opportunities in ministry.[15]

QUESTIONS TO CONSIDER

For the congregations in your list, please indicate which relationships involve each of the following: friendships between ministers, joint events, ministerial groups, and pulpit exchanges.

1. In your relationships with other congregations, what way of building relationships is most common, and what way of building relationships is least common—friendships between ministers, joint events, ministerial groups, or pulpit exchanges?
2. What ways of building relationships would you like to be more intentional about?
3. In your relationships with other congregations, what relationship type is most common, and what relationship type is least common—within religious group, between religious groups, within racial group, or between racial groups?
4. What relationship types would you like to be more intentional about?
5. What practical advice can you use from this book to identify types of relationships that may be beneficial for your congregation and to build these relationships?

Appendix

Getting to Know the Social Network of Central Alabama Congregations

In this appendix, I introduce how I gathered information from central Alabama congregations, the characteristics of these congregations, and how I created the network.

SURVEYING CENTRAL ALABAMA CONGREGATIONS

In 2017 and 2018, I collected data from central Alabama congregations through a survey completed by one person at the congregation—typically, a minister. All faith traditions were welcome to participate in the survey. This survey asked questions about a wide variety of topics in congregational life, including religious or denominational affiliation, founding date, location, attendance, worship and cultural styles, characteristics of attenders, characteristics of leaders and staff, financial and human resources, facilities, vitality, challenges, and connections with other congregations, parachurch ministries, and nonprofit organizations.

The study area was limited to eight central Alabama counties: Bibb, Blount, Cullman, Jefferson, St. Clair, Shelby, Tuscaloosa, and Walker. I present a map of these counties later in this appendix. In 2017, Samford's Center for Congregational Resources mailed surveys to all of the congregations we were aware of in these counties. In 2018, I invited congregations to participate in a phone interview that included the same questions as the printed questionnaires. To make sure that there was interconnectedness within the network, I limited eligibility for the phone interviews to only congregations that had been mentioned by a participating congregation as being a connection. Overall, 438 congregations participated in this survey, 171 through the mailed survey and 267 through a phone interview. In addition, 639 congregations were mentioned as a connection by a participating congregation but did not participate in the survey. Overall, of the congregations I am aware of in these eight counties, 20 percent (438 of 2,186) participated in the survey, and 29 percent (639 of 2,186) were mentioned as a connection but did not participate. I present more information about the data collection in my article "Connected and Fragmented: Introducing a Social Network Study of Religious Congregations."[1]

INTRODUCING CENTRAL ALABAMA CONGREGATIONS

In this section, I describe the 438 congregations that participated in the survey. For each characteristic described below, I also include the number of congregations that answered that question since congregations were able to skip questions that they did not want to answer.

Table A.1. Cultural Characteristics of the Surveyed Congregations

Denominational Affiliation?		Religious Family	
Yes	81%	Anglican/Episcopal	3%
No	19%	Baptist	34%
N=437		Congregationalist	1%
		Eastern Orthodox	<1%
Racial Composition		Holiness	3%
Non-Hispanic White	70%	Independent Fundamentalist	<1%
African American	20%	Jewish	1%
Hispanic/Latino	<1%	Latter-day Saints	3%
Asian/Pacific Islander	<1%	Lutheran	2%
Other	<1%	Methodist	15%
Multiracial	9%	Muslim	<1%
N=429		Pentecostal	15%
		Presbyterian	8%
Religious Tradition		Quaker	<1%
Black Protestant	17%	Restoration	4%
Evangelical Protestant	54%	Roman Catholic	4%
Mainline Protestant	19%	Seventh-day Adventist	1%
Roman Catholic	4%	Spiritualist	<1%
Other	5%	Unitarian Universalist	<1%
N=438		Not clear	4%
		N=438	

Cultures

Table A.1 presents information about the congregations' cultures.

There are different approaches for understanding and categorizing religious and denominational identities, and this appendix uses three to do so. First, we can look at whether congregations are formally affiliated with a denomination, convention, or some similar kind of association. In this study, about 80 percent have a denominational affiliation, and about 20 percent do not.

The second approach involves classifying congregations by historical and theological families.[2] The size of each family among this study's participants and the most common denominations and groups within each family are presented below. The families are listed below by size from largest to smallest.

- In this study a third of the congregations are in the Baptist family, and the most common denominations are the Southern Baptist Convention, a predominantly non-Hispanic white, conservative denomination that is the largest Protestant denomination in the United States; the National Baptist Convention, USA, Inc., a predominantly African American denomination; the Cooperative Baptist Fellowship, a moderate-to-progressive Baptist denomination; and Primitive Baptists, a group of nondenominational Calvinist congregations.
- Fifteen percent are in the Pentecostal family. Over 60 percent of the congregations in this study that are from this family are nondenominational and described themselves as being Charismatic and/or as incorporating speaking in tongues into their religious services. The most common Pentecostal denomination in this study is the Church of God (Cleveland, TN).
- Another 15 percent are in the Methodist family. The most common Methodist denominations in this study are the United Methodist Church, a moderate to progressive denomination that is the second largest Protestant denomination in the United States; two predominantly African American denominations, the African Methodist Episcopal Church and the Christian Methodist Episcopal Church; and the Bible Methodist Connection of Churches, a more theologically conservative denomination.
- Eight percent are in the Presbyterian family. The most common Presbyterian denominations in this study are the Presbyterian Church (U.S.A.), a more progressive denomination; the Presbyterian Church in America, a more theologically conservative denomination; the Cumberland Presbyterian Church, which historically adopted a model of itinerancy similar to the Methodists and is not as Calvinist as other Presbyterian denominations.

- Four percent are Roman Catholic. The Roman Catholic Church is the largest religious body in the United States.
- Another 4 percent are from the Restoration family. There are two Restoration groups in this study: the Christian Church/Disciples of Christ, a moderate to progressive denomination, and the theologically conservative, nondenominational, and noninstrumental Churches of Christ.
- Three percent are in the Holiness family. Holiness denominations include the Church of the Nazarene, the Church of God (Anderson, IN), the Christian and Missionary Alliance, and the Wesleyan Church.
- Three percent are Anglican/Episcopal. In the United States, the Episcopal Church is more theologically progressive, and Anglican churches tend to be more theologically conservative.
- An additional 3 percent are from the Latter-day Saint family and particularly from the Church of Jesus Christ of Latter-day Saints.
- Two percent are in the Lutheran family. Lutheran denominations in this study include the more mainline Evangelical Lutheran Church in America, the more conservative Lutheran Church–Missouri Synod, and the more moderate Lutheran Congregations in Mission for Christ.
- Each of the remaining families make up 1 percent or less of this study's congregations: Congregationalist (e.g., United Church of Christ), Eastern Orthodox, Independent Fundamentalist, Jewish, Muslim, Quaker, Seventh-day Adventist, Spiritualist, and Unitarian Universalist.

In addition, 4 percent of participating congregations have a religious family that is not clear.[3]

The third approach uses denominational and nondenominational identities as well as racial composition to categorize Protestant congregations into three traditions. Because this scheme incorporates racial composition, here's a brief description of the racial compositions of this study's congregations. Seventy percent of congregations are predominantly non-Hispanic white, 20% are predominantly African American, 1% are predominantly another racial or ethnic group, and 9% are multiracial with no racial group making up at least 80% of regular attenders.[4] Both denomination and racial composition are used to define the first Protestant tradition.

- Black Protestant—Many scholars define Black Protestantism as a separate Protestant tradition because it has a central role in African American communities, civil rights, and racial justice movements, as well as a stronger emphasis on freedom, liberation, and justice. This group includes congregations from traditionally African American denominations, like the National Baptist Convention, USA, Inc., the African

Methodist Episcopal Church, and the Christian Methodist Episcopal Church, as well as Baptist, Methodist, and nondenominational congregations that are at least 80 percent African American.

- Evangelical Protestant—Evangelical Protestant denominations are typically more theologically conservative and exclusive, with focuses on individual relationships with Christ, missions, and evangelism. The most common Evangelical Protestant denominations in this study include the Southern Baptist Convention, the Church of God (Cleveland, TN), the Presbyterian Church in America, the Church of the Nazarene, and the Cumberland Presbyterian Church. There are many nondenominational congregations in this category as well.
- Mainline Protestant—Mainline Protestant denominations are typically more theologically liberal and inclusive, with stronger orientations toward social justice and more appreciation for religious diversity. The most common Mainline Protestant denominations in this study include the United Methodist Church, the Episcopal Church, the Presbyterian Church (U.S.A.), the Christian Church/Disciples of Christ, and the United Church of Christ.

In addition to these groups, there are also categories for Roman Catholic congregations as well as congregations from other traditions, including Eastern Orthodox, Jewish, Latter-day Saint, Muslim, Spiritualist, and Unitarian Universalist.[5] Over half of the congregations in this study are Evangelical Protestant, 19% are Mainline Protestant, 17% are Black Protestant, 4% are Roman Catholic, and 5% are from other traditions.

Locations

There are a variety of factors through which we can understand congregations' locations, including their county of location, their community type, the racial composition of their neighborhood, and the economic characteristics of their neighborhood. This information regarding location was not asked of congregations but was ascertained using Geographic Information Systems (GIS).[6] Key information about congregations' locations is presented in table A.2, and a map of the eight-county study area is presented in figure A.1.

Congregations come from a variety of counties and community types. About half of the congregations in the study are in Jefferson County, which includes the city of Birmingham and part of the city of Hoover, as well as surrounding suburbs, some small towns, and rural communities. Fifteen percent of the congregations are in Shelby County, which includes part of the city of Hoover, many suburbs, some small towns, and rural communities. Twelve percent are from Tuscaloosa County, which includes the city of Tuscaloosa,

Table A.2. Locations of the Surveyed Congregations

County		Percentage Non-Hispanic White*		Below Poverty Level*	
Bibb	1%	Less than 20%	14%	Less than 5%	11%
Blount	4%	20–39.9%	9%	5–9.9%	20%
Cullman	6%	40–59.9%	9%	10–19.9%	34%
Jefferson	51%	60–79.9%	26%	20–29.9%	16%
Shelby	15%	80–89.9%	20%	30–39.9%	9%
St. Clair	6%	90–100%	22%	At least 40%	10%
Tuscaloosa	12%	N=438		N=438	
Walker	6%				
N=438		Percentage African American*		Median household income*	
		Less than 5%	27%	Less than $25,000	10%
Community Type		5–9.9%	14%	$25,000–$34,999	16%
City	29%	10–19.9%	21%	$35,000–$49,999	28%
Suburb	39%	20–49.9%	13%	$50,000–$69,999	24%
Town	8%	50–79.9%	12%	$70,000–$99,999	14%
Rural	24%	80–100%	13%	$100,000 or higher	7%
N=438		N=438		N=438	

*in Census tract

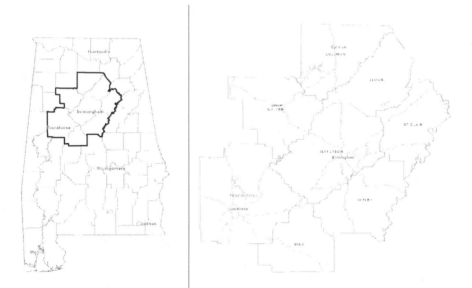

Figure A.1. Map of Central Alabama Study Area. Created by the author using ArcGIS with assistance from Jonathan Fleming.

the home of the University of Alabama, as well as suburbs, small towns, and rural communities. Less than 25% of this study's congregations are in the five remaining counties, which are primarily made up of small towns and rural communities: Bibb, Blount, Cullman, St. Clair, and Walker counties. Overall, 29% of this study's congregations are in urban settings, 39% are in suburbs, 8% are in small towns, and 24% are in rural communities.

The congregations also differ in the racial and economic characteristics of their Census tracts. Because of the significant racial white/African American residential segregation in the study area, the description of the racial compositions focuses on the percentage of residents who are non-Hispanic white or African American. About half of the congregations are in largely racially homogeneous communities. About 40% of the congregations are located in a Census tract that is at least 80% non-Hispanic white and where less than 10% of residents are African American. In addition, 12% of congregations are located in a Census tract that is at least 80% African American and where less than 10% of residents are non-Hispanic white. Only about 12% of congregations are located in Census tracts where no racial or ethnic group makes up 60% or more of residents. There is also a wide range of poverty levels and household incomes among the communities in which the congregations are located. The income level below which a person is in poverty is defined based on a household's size. In 2018 a household of four people was considered to be in poverty if their income was under $25,100. About 30% of congregations are in a Census tract with a poverty level of less than 10%, 50% are in Census tract with a poverty level of 10–29.9%, and about 20% are in Census tract with a poverty level of at least 30%. For median household income, about a quarter of congregations are in Census tracts with median household incomes of less than $35,000; over half are in Census tracts with median household incomes of $35,000–$69,999; and about 20% are in Census tracts with median household incomes of $70,000 or more.[7]

Other Characteristics

Table A.3 presents ten additional characteristics of this study's congregations. The first three concern congregation size, founding, and structure. Over 40% of this study's congregations have an average weekly attendance of fewer than one hundred, and just over 10% have an average weekly attendance of five hundred or more. The participating congregations have a range of founding dates. Almost half were founded before 1950, and about 20% were founded since 2000. Only 3% of the participating congregations are multisite, having worship services at multiple locations, all of which are considered part of the same congregation. The next three characteristics concern regularly attending adults at the participating congregations. Congregations differ in the percentages of regularly attending adults that are sixty or older, younger than thirty-five, and new in the past five years. A typical congregation would lean toward having more older adults, fewer young adults, and fewer new adults. The final four characteristics concern the main minister (or the solo or leading minister, pastor, priest, rabbi, imam, etc.). Most congregations (92%) have a male main minister, and 8% of congregations have a female main minister. There is a wide range of ages among the main ministers, with most being between forty and sixty-four years old. The main ministers also have varying tenures at their congregations, and 60% have a tenure of less than ten years. Levels of theological education also differ between the main ministers. Over 60% have a graduate degree, while 25% have either no or certificate-level theological education.

Table A.3. Other Characteristics of the Surveyed Congregations

Average Weekly Attendance		Regularly Attending Adults, Age 60+		Main Minister's Sex	
Under 50	21%	0–10%	13%	Female	8%
50–99	23%	11–20%	14%	Male	92%
100–199	23%	21–40%	35%	N=437	
200–349	14%	41–60%	27%		
350–499	7%	61–100%	12%	Main Minister's Age	
500–999	6%	N=436		Under 40	14%
1,000–1,999	3%			40–54	35%
2,000+	2%	Regularly Attending Adults, Age <35		55–64	34%
N=438		0–10%	20%	65+	17%
		11–20%	20%	N=437	
Founding Date		21–40%	43%		
Before 1900	26%	41–60%	12%	Main Minister's Tenure at Location	
1900–1949	22%	61–100%	5%		
1950–1979	19%	N=436		Under 5 years	40%
1980–1999	12%			5–9 years	20%
2000 or later	21%			10–19 years	26%
N=435		Regularly Attending Adults, New 5 Yrs		20+ years	14%
		0–10%	21%	N=437	
		11–20%	29%		
		21–40%	30%	Main Minister's Theology Education	
Multisite		41–60%	9%		
Yes	3%	61–100%	11%	None	11%
No	97%	N=436		Certificate	14%
N=437				Bachelor's degree	11%
				Master's degree	42%
				Doctoral degree	21%
				N=433	

CREATING A SOCIAL NETWORK OF
CENTRAL ALABAMA CONGREGATIONS

In the survey, congregations were asked to mention up to ten congregations within the study area with whom they had connections. For each congregation mentioned, participating congregations were also asked to describe the type(s) of relationships. Options included joint events such as religious services, service projects, and conferences or retreats; friendships with ministers from other congregations; participating in a clergy peer group or a ministerial association with ministers from other congregations; and exchanging pulpits with ministers from other congregations. In creating the network, I consider relationships to be present among a pair of congregations if either mentioned any type of relationship, and absent if neither mentioned a relationship. I present more information about measuring relational ties in my article "Connected and Fragmented: Introducing a Social Network Study of Religious Congregations."[8]

There are two important decisions in measuring relationships between congregations that are important to keep in mind throughout this book. First, congregations were limited to reporting at most ten connections with other congregations. When doing a survey, it is important to find a balance between collecting enough information to make the study worthwhile and not making the survey so long that congregations are discouraged from participating. Network questions typically are complex and take a lot of time, and this was certainly the case in this study. Participants needed to list congregations by name, give enough information so that I could differentiate between congregations with similar names, and then describe the types of relationships with each of the congregations mentioned. Almost 20 percent of the congregations that participated mentioned ten connections, and some of them certainly would have mentioned more connections if I had let them. So, in the network presented in this book, there are not congregations with direct connections to dozens of congregations, and this is why.

Second, congregations were limited to mentioning congregations within the eight-county study area. To illustrate why, here's an example of what might have happened if I had not limited congregations in this way. Let's consider a situation where a participating congregation mentioned connections not only with congregations within the study area but also with congregations in Atlanta, Nashville, Louisville, Peru, and the Dominican Republic. I would have then needed to reach out to these congregations and invite them to participate in the survey. If some of these congregations participated and mentioned congregations both in their communities and in additional communities, then I would have needed to reach out to even more congregations from different communities around the United States and the world. Allowing congregations to mention connections outside of the study area would have quickly increased this study's scope and made the study unfeasible to conduct. However, it is important to keep in mind that many of the participating congregations have meaningful relationships with congregations outside of the study area.

Using the relationships mentioned by congregations, I created several social network diagrams, which I present throughout the book. Each circle represents a congregation that participated in the 2017–2018 survey. Lines represent relationships, and lines are present if, for a pair of congregations, one or both of the congregations mentioned at least one type of relationship. In these figures, I organize the network into clusters using a procedure that maximizes relationships within clusters and minimizes them between clusters.[9] I do this so that the network images don't look like a jumbled bowl of spaghetti. (If you think the images look like a bowl of spaghetti anyway, that's fine. It's just even messier if I don't use clusters.)

I'd like to describe the relational patterns related to religious group and race in table A.4, and I need to introduce a few technical terms to do so. The first technical term is an *alter*, which is a congregation (congregation A) to which another congregation (congregation B) has a direct relational tie through, for example, a friendship between the ministers or a joint event. The terminology of an alter is important for understanding the second term—*homophily*, or the dynamic where "birds of a feather flock together."[10] It is well documented among individuals; individuals are more likely to be friends and romantic partners (that is, *alters*) with people who are similar in race, gender (for friendships), age, religion, education and economic level, and attitudes and beliefs. Homophily also occurs among congregations, and there are more likely to be relationships between congregations (or, in other words, congregations are more likely to be alters) when they share the same religious group or racial composition.[11] In this study, homophily can only be measured for alters that participated in the survey.[12] The first type of homophily involves sharing the same religious group. Thirty-two percent of congregations have only alters that share their religious group, another 32% have at least half but not all alters that share their religious group, 19% have some but less than half of alters that share their religious group, and 17% have no alters that share their religious group. The second type of homophily focuses on whether congregations share the same racial composition. About half of the congregations have only alters that share their racial composition, about 30% have at least half but not all alters that share their racial composition, 7% have some but less than half of alters that share their racial composition, and 12% have no alters that share their racial composition.

Table A.4. Network Characteristics of the Surveyed Congregations

Alters with the Same Religious Group		Alters with the Same Racial Composition	
0%	17%	0%	12%
1–49%	19%	1–49%	7%
50–99%	32%	50–99%	31%
100%	32%	100%	49%
N=407		N=407	

INTERVIEWS WITH MINISTERS AND LEADERS

In the summer and fall of 2021, I reinterviewed fifty ministers and leaders about their congregations' opportunities and challenges and how their relationships with other congregations helped them to navigate these situations. I present many of their stories throughout this book. Table A.5 presents the breakdown of religious groups and counties among congregations that participated in interviews.

Table A.5. Characteristics of the Interviewed Congregations

Religious Group	N	County	N
American Fellowship of Cowboy Churches	1	Bibb	0
Christian Methodist Episcopal Church	2	Blount	2
Church of Christ	3	Cullman	3
Church of Jesus Christ of Latter-day Saints	2	Jefferson	30
Cooperative Baptist Fellowship	1	Shelby	3
Eastern Orthodox	1	St. Clair	2
Episcopal Church	1	Tuscaloosa	9
Independent Fundamentalist	1	Walker	1
Jewish	1		50
Muslim	1		
National Baptist Convention of America	1		
National Baptist Convention, USA, Inc.	7		
Nondenominational	8		
Presbyterian Church (U.S.A.)	2		
Presbyterian Church In America	2		
Roman Catholic	2		
Seventh-day Adventist Church	1		
Southern Baptist Convention	11		
United Methodist Church	2		
	50		

Notes

PREFACE

1. Thomas Merton, *No Man Is an Island* (New York: Harcourt, 1955), xxii.

CHAPTER 1

1. For a helpful book on how congregations can navigate anxious times in healthy ways, see Peter L. Steinke, *Uproar: Calm Leadership in Anxious Times* (Lanham, MD: Rowman & Littlefield, 2019). Social support has helped individuals in difficult situations to cope with stress in healthy ways, and relationships and social support within congregations are particularly helpful for promoting healthy coping; see James S. House, Debra Umberson, and Kark R. Landis, "Structures and Processes of Social Support," *Annual Review of Sociology* 14 (1988); Neal Krause et al., "Church-Based Social Support and Religious Coping," *Journal for the Scientific Study of Religion* 40, no. 4 (2001).

2. For selected findings from the 2021 Pew Research survey, see Gregory A. Smith, "About Three-In-Ten U.S. Adults Are Now Religiously Unaffiliated," Pew Research Center, published December 14, 2021, https://www.pewresearch.org/religion/2021/12/14/about-three-in-ten-u-s-adults-are-now-religiously-unaffiliated/. For additional information about religious "nones," see Mark Chaves, *American Religion: Contemporary Trends*, 2nd ed. (Princeton, NJ: Princeton University Press, 2017), 14, 45; Pew Research Center, "In U.S., Decline of Christianity Continues at Rapid Pace," published October 17, 2019, https://www.pewforum.org/2019/10/17/in-u-s-decline-of-christianity-continues-at-rapid-pace/; and Pew Research Center, "'Nones' on the Rise," published October 9, 2012, https://www.pewforum.org/2012/10/09/nones-on-the-rise/. For more information on the decline of U.S. Christian denominations, see Bob Smietana, *Reorganized Religion: The Reshaping of the American Church and Why It Matters* (New York: Worthy Publishing, 2022), 3–32.

3. For the percentage of millennials who are not religious, see Pew Research Center, "In U.S., Decline of Christianity Continues at Rapid Pace." For data on the percentage of millennials who attend at least once a month and the increasing age

of attenders, see Chaves, *American Religion*, 51, 66–67. For innovative strategies for nurturing the faith of youth and young adults, see the following: Scott Cormode, *The Innovative Church: How Leaders and Their Congregations Can Adapt in an Ever-Changing World* (Grand Rapids, MI: Baker Academic, 2020); Kara Powell, Jake Mulder, and Brad Griffin, *Growing Young: 6 Essential Strategies to Help Young People Discover and Love Your Church* (Grand Rapids, MI: Baker Books, 2016).

4. Yonat Shimron, "Study: Attendance Hemorrhaging at Small and Midsize U.S. Congregations," *Religion News Service*, October 14, 2021, https://religionnews.com/2021/10/14/study-attendance-at-small-and-midsize-us-congregations-is-hemorrhaging/.

5. Chaves, *American Religion*, 73.

6. For information on the concentration of attenders into larger congregations, see Chaves, *American Religion*, 72–74; Smietana, *Reorganized Religion*, 102–18.

7. Nancy T. Ammerman, *Congregation and Community* (New Brunswick, NJ: Rutgers University Press, 1997).

8. For research on American political polarization, see Michael Dimock and Richard Wike, "America Is Exceptional in Its Political Divide," *Pew Trust Magazine*, March 29, 2021, https://www.pewtrusts.org/en/trust/archive/winter-2021/america-is-exceptional-in-its-political-divide; Pew Research Center, "Voters' Attitudes About Race and Gender Are Even More Divided Than in 2016," published September 10, 2020, https://www.pewresearch.org/politics/2020/09/10/voters-attitudes-about-race-and-gender-are-even-more-divided-than-in-2016/. For political topics in sermons, see Matthew Brown, "Pew Analysis: Sermons Turned to Political Messaging in 2020 amid Election, Protests, COVID-19," *USA Today*, July 11, 2021, https://www.usatoday.com/story/news/politics/2021/07/11/pew-analysis-sermons-turned-political-2020-amid-covid-election/7930097002/. For information about polarization related to worship service attendance, see Chaves, *American Religion*, 101–16. For interesting research on Christian nationalism, see Andrew L. Whitehead and Samuel L. Perry, *Taking America Back for God: Christian Nationalism in the United States* (New York: Oxford University Press, 2020). For data on the growing opposition to religious influence in politics, see Chaves, *American Religion*, 114–16. For information about the political preferences of young adults and nonreligious people, see Pew Research Center, "In U.S., Decline of Christianity Continues at Rapid Pace"; Pew Research Center, "The Generation Gap in American Politics," published March 1, 2018, https://www.pewresearch.org/politics/2018/03/01/the-generation-gap-in-american-politics/. For more information on how polarization is impacting religious decline in America, see Smietana, *Reorganized Religion*, 119–39.

9. For research on how much time congregational ministers invest in their ministry and its impact on their health, see Jackson W. Carroll, *God's Potters: Pastoral Leadership and the Shaping of Congregations* (Grand Rapids, MI: William B. Eerdmans Publishing, 2006), 96–126; Cynthia Woolever and Deborah Bruce, *Leadership That Fits Your Church: What Kind of Pastor for What Kind of Congregation* (St. Louis, MO: Chalice Press, 2012), 51–65; and Rae Jean Proeschold-Bell and Jason Byassee, *Faithful and Fractured: Responding to the Clergy Health Crisis* (Grand Rapids, MI: Baker Academic, 2018). For research on declining confidence in religious leaders, see Chaves, *American Religion*, 81–87.

10. Claire Gecewicz, "Few Americans Say Their House of Worship Is Open, But a Quarter Say Their Faith Has Grown amid Pandemic," Pew Research Center, published April 30, 2020, https://www.pewresearch.org/fact-tank/2020/04/30/few-americans-say-their-house-of-worship-is-open-but-a-quarter-say-their-religious-faith-has-grown-amid-pandemic/.

11. Adelle M. Banks, "Amid COVID-19, Most Churches Provide Hybrid Worship, Half Stopped Picnics," *Religion News Service*, November 10, 2021, https://religionnews.com/2021/11/10/amid-covid-19-most-churches-provide-hybrid-worship-half-stopped-picnics/.

12. Elizabeth Felicetti, "My Church Doesn't Know What to Do Anymore," *The Atlantic*, October 27, 2021, https://www.theatlantic.com/ideas/archive/2021/10/church-pandemic/620496/.

13. Banks, "Amid COVID-19."

14. For pandemic-related community service by congregations, see Banks, "Amid COVID-19"; Adelle M. Banks, "Churches' Ministry to Those Hurt by the Pandemic Shows 'Monumental' Growth, Study Says," *Religion News Service*, December 21, 2021, https://religionnews.com/2021/12/21/churches-adapt-social-ministries-even-as-they-lose-members-to-the-pandemic/; and Hartford Institute for Religion Research, *Congregational Response to the Pandemic: Extraordinary Social Outreach in a Time of Crisis* (Hartford, CT: Hartford Institute for Religion Research, 2021), https://www.covidreligionresearch.org/wp-content/uploads/2021/12/Congregational-Response-to-the-Pandemic_Extraordinary-Social-Outreach-in-a-Time-of-Crisis_Dec-2021.pdf. For more information about models of community ministry, see Joy F. Skjegstad, *7 Creative Models for Community Ministry* (Valley Forge, PA: Judson Press, 2013).

15. Elizabeth E. Evans, "For Clergy, COVID-19 Has Brought Both Burnout and Breakthrough," *Religion News Service*, February 21, 2022, https://religionnews.com/2022/02/21/for-clergy-covid-19-has-brought-both-burnout-and-breakthrough/.

16. See Banks, "Amid COVID-19"; Hartford Institute for Religion Research, *Navigating the Pandemic: A First Look at Congregational Responses* (Hartford, CT: Hartford Institute for Religion Research, 2021), https://www.covidreligionresearch.org/wp-content/uploads/2021/11/Navigating-the-Pandemic_A-First-Look-at-Congregational-Responses_Nov-2021.pdf. For information on full-time ministers leaving ministry, see Michelle Boorstein, "The First Christmas as a Layperson: Burned Out by the Pandemic, Many Clergy Quit in the Past Year," *Washington Post*, December 24, 2021, https://www.washingtonpost.com/religion/2021/12/24/christmas-covid-pandemic-clergy-quit/; Barna Group, "38% of U.S. Pastors Have Thought About Quitting Full-Time Ministry in the Past Year," updated 2021, https://www.barna.com/research/pastors-well-being/; and Scott Thumma, "Is a Great Resignation Brewing for Pastors?" *Religion News Service*, March 18, 2022, https://religionnews.com/2022/03/18/is-a-great-resignation-brewing-for-pastors/.

17. Scott Thumma, "The Pandemic Impact on Congregations: What Do We Know and What Still Needs to Be Learned?" (presentation, Lilly Endowment's Thriving Congregations Annual Gathering, Indianapolis, IN, October 10–12, 2022). See also Smietana, *Reorganized Religion*, 65–78, for an overview of how the COVID-19 pandemic has impacted religious decline in the United States.

18. For types of social support, see Catherine P. H. Langford et al., "Social Support: A Conceptual Analysis," *Journal of Advanced Nursing* 25 (1997): 96–97; Shelley E. Taylor, "Social Support: A Review," in *The Oxford Handbook of Health Psychology*, ed. Howard S. Friedman (New York: Oxford University Press, 2011), 192–93. There is also a fourth type of social support. "Appraisal support involves the communication of information which is relevant to self-evaluation, rather than problem-solving," according to Langford et al., "Social Support," 97. "Appraisal support should be used sparingly and only in a context where people know each other really well and have a deep enough trust in the other person's kind intention that [they] can receive information that helps with self-evaluation that will not be experienced as just criticism," according to Emily Nagoski and Amelia Nagoski, "Episode 31: Social Support," May 17, 2020, in the *Feminist Survival Project 2020*, podcast, MP3 audio, 39:36, https://www.feministsurvivalproject.com/episodes/episode-31-social-support. None of the ministers and leaders I interviewed for this book mentioned offering or receiving appraisal support.

19. For an examination of relationship types between congregations, see Jennifer M. McClure, "Connected and Fragmented: Introducing a Social Network Study of Religious Congregations," *Interdisciplinary Journal of Research on Religion* 16, no. 4 (2020). For information on ministerial associations, see Nancy T. Ammerman, *Pillars of Faith: American Congregations and Their Partners* (Berkeley, CA: University of California Press, 2005), 111–12. For information on clergy peer groups, see Penny Long Marler et al., *So Much Better: How Thousands of Pastors Help Each Other Thrive* (St. Louis, MO: Chalice Press, 2013).

20. Proeschold-Bell and Byassee, *Faithful and Fractured*, 29

21. Proeschold-Bell and Byassee, *Faithful and Fractured*, 128.

22. For more research on clergy health, see Woolever and Bruce, *Leadership That Fits Your Church*; Proeschold-Bell and Byassee, *Faithful and Fractured*. For a wonderful book about burnout and caring for each other in the midst of it, see Emily Nagoski and Amelia Nagoski, *Burnout: The Secret to Unlocking the Stress Cycle* (New York: Ballantine Books, 2019).

23. Proeschold-Bell and Byassee, *Faithful and Fractured*, 128.

24. Carroll, *God's Potters*, 212.

25. For research on the impact of clergy peer groups in congregational life, see Marler et al., *So Much Better*, 7–8.

26. For definitions of and research on homophily, a network dynamic where relationships are more common when a similarity is shared, see Miller McPherson, Lynn Smith-Lovin, and James M. Cook, "Birds of a Feather: Homophily in Social Networks," *Annual Review of Sociology* 27 (2001); Jeffrey A. Smith, Miller McPherson, and Lynn Smith-Lovin, "Social Distance in the United States: Sex, Race, Religion, Age, and Education Homophily among Confidants, 1985 to 2004," *American Sociological Review* 79, no. 3 (2014). The quote "birds of a feather flock together" comes from Thomas Rotolo and J. Miller McPherson, "The System of Occupations: Modeling Occupations in Sociodemographic Space," *Social Forces* 79, no. 3 (2001): 1101. For research on homophily in this network of congregations, see Jennifer M. McClure, "Congregations of a Feather? Exploring Homophily in a Network of

Religious Congregations," *Review of Religious Research* 63, no. 4 (2021). For information about ministers' work schedules, see Carroll, *God's Potters*, 96–126. For the convenience of denomination networks for building relationships with other congregations, ministers, and leaders, see McClure, "Congregations of a Feather," 578. For advantages of high homophily, see Yannick C. Atouba and Michelle Shumate, "International Nonprofit Collaboration: Examining the Role of Homophily," *Nonprofit and Voluntary Sector Quarterly* 44, no. 3 (2015): 603; Oluwaseun Akinyemi, Bronwyn Harris, and Mary Kawonga, "Innovation Diffusion: How Homogeneous Networks Influence the Uptake of Community-Based Injectable Contraceptives," *BMC Public Health* 19 (2019).

27. For research about the benefits of tight-knit relationships, see Gautam Ahuja, "Collaboration Networks, Structural Holes, and Innovation: A Longitudinal Study," *Administrative Science Quarterly* 45 (2000); Andrew V. Shipilov and Stan Xiao Li, "Can You Have Your Cake and Eat It Too? Structural Holes' Influence on Status Accumulation and Market Performance in Collaborative Networks," *Administrative Science Quarterly* 53 (2008): 101; and Giuseppe Soda, Alessandro Usai, and Akbar Zaheer, "Network Memory: The Influence of Past and Current Networks on Performance," *The Academy of Management Journal* 47, no. 6 (2004): 896. For research on the disadvantages of tight-knit relationships, see Akbar Zaheer and Geoffrey G. Bell, "Benefiting from Network Position: Firm Capabilities, Structural Holes, and Performance," *Strategic Management Journal* 26, no. 9 (2005): 814; Martin Gargiulo and Mario Benassi, "Trapped in Your Own Net? Network Cohesion, Structural Holes, and the Adaptation of Social Capital," *Organization Science* 11, no. 2 (2000): 193.

28. For information on the disadvantages of high homophily, see Atouba and Shumate, "International Nonprofit Collaboration," 603. For information on homophily and the importance of bridges, see Mark Granovetter, "The Strength of Weak Ties: A Network Theory Revisited," *Sociological Theory* 1 (1983): 204, 215. For the impact of homophily on information diffusion, see Neha Gondal, "Inequality Preservation through Uneven Diffusion of Cultural Materials across Stratified Groups," *Social Forces* 93, no. 3 (2015). For information on "weak ties" across differences, see Mark Granovetter, "The Strength of Weak Ties," *American Journal of Sociology* 78, no. 6 (1973); Granovetter, "The Strength of Weak Ties: A Network Theory Revisited."

29. For more information about racial homophily among central Alabama congregations, see McClure, "Congregations of a Feather." For information about the racial compositions of U.S. religious groups, see Michael Lipka, "The Most and Least Racially Diverse U.S. Religious Groups," Pew Research Center, published July 27, 2015, https://www.pewresearch.org/fact-tank/2015/07/27/the-most-and-least-racially -diverse-u-s-religious-groups/.

30. For information on the advantages of diverse relationships for collaborations, see Atouba and Shumate, "International Nonprofit Collaboration," 603. For dynamics related to single versus multiple racial cultures in a congregation, see Michael O. Emerson and Christian Smith, *Divided by Faith: Evangelical Religion and the Problem of Race in America* (New York: Oxford University Press, 2000), 145–48.

31. For Alabama's voting in the 2020 presidential election, see Politico, "Alabama Presidential Results," accessed November 4, 2022, https://www.politico.com/2020

-election/results/alabama/. For education rankings, see "Education Rankings," U.S. News & World Report, accessed November 4, 2022, https://www.usnews.com/news/best-states/rankings/education. For poverty rates, see John Creamer et al., *Poverty in the United States: 2021* (Washington, DC: U.S. Census Bureau, 2022), https://www.census.gov/content/dam/Census/library/publications/2022/demo/p60-277.pdf. For health outcomes, see "Health Care Rankings," U.S. News & World Report, accessed November 4, 2022, https://www.usnews.com/news/best-states/rankings/health-care; "Public Health Rankings," U.S. News & World Report, accessed November 4, 2022, https://www.usnews.com/news/best-states/rankings/health-care/public-health. For data on the religious composition of Alabama and the study area, see "U.S. Congregational Membership Reports," Association of Religion Data Archives, accessed November 8, 2022, https://thearda.com/us-religion/census/congregational-membership; "U.S. State Maps," Association of Religion Data Archives, accessed November 8, 2022, https://thearda.com/us-religion/maps/us-state-maps.

32. For more information on Birmingham's steel industry, see Jack Bergstresser, "Iron and Steel Production in Birmingham," Encyclopedia of Alabama, accessed November 4, 2022, http://encyclopediaofalabama.org/Article/h-1638#:~:text=In%20the%20decades%20after%20the,in%20the%20southern%20United%20States. For the most segregated U.S. cities, see "Most to Least Segregated Cities," Othering and Belonging Institute, accessed November 4, 2022, https://belonging.berkeley.edu/most-least-segregated-cities. For information about the bombing of Sixteenth Street Baptist Church, see "16th Street Baptist Church Bombing (1963)," National Park Service, accessed November 4, 2022, https://www.nps.gov/articles/16thstreetbaptist.htm. For information about civil rights in Birmingham, see "Birmingham Civil Rights Institute," U.S. Civil Rights Trail, accessed November 4, 2022, https://civilrightstrail.com/attraction/birmingham-civil-rights-institute/; Martin Luther King Jr., *Letter from Birmingham Jail* (London: Penguin, 2018). For more information about Birmingham's economy, see "Birmingham: Economy," City-Data, accessed November 4, 2022, https://www.city-data.com/us-cities/The-South/Birmingham-Economy.html. For the University of Alabama at Birmingham Hospital, see Bob Shepard, "UAB Hospital Now Eighth-Largest in the Nation," *UAB News*, December 7, 2021, https://www.uab.edu/news/health/item/12492-uab-hospital-now-eighth-largest-in-the-nation. For information about the World Games of 2022 in Birmingham, see Kyra Miles, "The World Games Kicks Off in Birmingham," *WBHM*, July 7, 2022, https://wbhm.org/2022/the-world-games-kicks-off-in-birmingham/. For some award-winning Birmingham restaurants, see Mary Colurso, "James Beard Awards: 7 Birmingham Restaurants and Chefs Honored by 'Oscars of the Food World,'" *AL.com*, July 31, 2022, https://www.al.com/life/2022/07/james-beard-awards-7-birmingham-restaurants-and-chefs-honored-by-oscars-of-the-food-world.html.

33. For more information about the history of Tuscaloosa, AL, see "History of Tuscaloosa," City of Tuscaloosa, accessed November 4, 2022, https://www.tuscaloosa.com/history. For information about George Wallace's actions at the University of Alabama, see Library of Congress, "Governor George Wallace Attempting to Block Integration at the University of Alabama," Prints and Photographs Online Catalog,

accessed November 7, 2022, https://www.loc.gov/pictures/item/2003688161/. On April 27, 2011, there were over one hundred tornadoes across the southern United States. "One of the cities hit hardest was Tuscaloosa, Ala." According to Tuscaloosa's mayor, "12% of the city was wiped out. Seven thousand people became unemployed within six minutes. . . . On top of that, we lost the Salvation Army and the American Red Cross." In addition, "the tornado also took out the county emergency management facility, communication towers, police cars, garbage trucks, and the sewage treatment plant—the very infrastructure necessary to respond in a disaster." Over a decade later, Tuscaloosa is still recovering from the tornado. For the quotes and details about the Tuscaloosa tornado, see Debbie Elliott, "'Day You'll Never Forget': Decade after Deadly Tuscaloosa Tornado, Recovery Is Uneven," *NPR*, April 27, 2021, https://www.npr.org/2021/04/27/991277578/day-youll-never-forget-decade-after-deadly-tuscaloosa-tornado-recovery-is-uneven. To explore the track of the tornado, see National Aeronautics and Space Administration, "Tuscaloosa Tornado Track Fades," NASA Earth Observatory, accessed November 7, 2022, https://earthobservatory.nasa.gov/images/87972/tuscaloosa-tornado-track-fades.

34. For an extensive overview of American religious groups, see J. Gordon Melton, *Melton's Encyclopedia of American Religions*, 8th ed. (Detroit, MI: Gale, 2009). For a racial breakdown of Alabama, see "QuickFacts Alabama; United States," U.S. Census Bureau, accessed November 7, 2022, https://www.census.gov/quickfacts/fact/table/AL,US/PST045221.

35. For reviews of literature on social support, see House, Umberson, and Landis, "Structures and Processes of Social Support"; Langford et al., "Social Support: A Conceptual Analysis"; and Taylor, "Social Support: A Review." There are about 106,000 scholarly articles that include "social support" in the title on Google Scholar. For a review of research on homophily, a network dynamic where relationships are more common when a similarity is shared, see McPherson, Smith-Lovin, and Cook, "Birds of a Feather." For research on homophily in this network of congregations, see McClure, "Congregations of a Feather." The quotes come, respectively, from Smith, McPherson, and Smith-Lovin, "Social Distance in the United States," 433; Gueorgi Kossinets and Duncan J. Watts, "Origins of Homophily in an Evolving Social Network," *American Journal of Sociology* 115, no. 2 (2009): 405.

36. The clusters were created using the Clauset-Newman-Moore algorithm, which maximizes relationships within clusters and minimizes them between clusters. For more information, see Aaron Clauset, M. E. J. Newman, and Cristopher Moore, "Finding Community Structure in Very Large Networks," *Physical Review E* 70, no. 6 (2004).

CHAPTER 2

1. For information about ministers' investment of time at their congregation and in their personal lives, see Carroll, *God's Potters*, 96–126. For information about how ministry impacts congregational ministers' personal lives, see Woolever and Bruce, *Leadership That Fits Your Church*, 55–56.

2. Homophily is a common feature of social networks, where relationships are more likely between two actors that share a similarity; see McPherson, Smith-Lovin, and Cook, "Birds of a Feather." For research on religious group/denominational homophily among congregations, see McClure, "Congregations of a Feather."

3. Primitive Baptist congregations and Church of Christ congregations are technically nondenominational, but I'm treating them as separate religious groups because their historical development and theology are distinctive from most nondenominational churches. See Melton, *Melton's Encyclopedia of American Religions.*

4. For information about denominational gatherings for clergy, see Ammerman, *Pillars of Faith*, 109.

5. For more information about the Association of Related Churches, see "About," Association of Related Churches, accessed January 28, 2022, https://www.arcchurches.com/about/.

6. See Granovetter, "The Strength of Weak Ties," 1361–62, for research on similarity and "strong ties."

7. For research on how similarities within relationships impacted the spread of contraceptive tools in Nigeria, see Akinyemi, Harris, and Kawonga, "Innovation Diffusion."

8. For research on how similarities impact collaborations between nongovernmental organizations, see Atouba and Shumate, "International Nonprofit Collaboration," 603.

9. Mary Fairchild, "How Does the Bible Define Discipleship?" Learn Religions, updated December 11, 2019, https://www.learnreligions.com/discipleship-definition-4132340.

10. "Baptist Faith and Message 2000," Southern Baptist Convention, accessed January 18, 2022, https://bfm.sbc.net/bfm2000/#xiv-cooperation.

11. "Serve," Serve Day, accessed March 7, 2022, https://serveday.com/.

12. Episcopal Church, "Peace, The," An Episcopal Dictionary of the Church, accessed January 28, 2022, https://www.episcopalchurch.org/glossary/peace-the/.

13. The American Fellowship of Cowboy Churches is a denomination with over 150 congregations. Most are in Texas, and there are twenty-one in Alabama. For more information, see "American Fellowship of Cowboy Churches," American Fellowship of Cowboy Churches, accessed November 1, 2022, https://americanfcc.org/.

CHAPTER 3

1. Melton, *Melton's Encyclopedia of American Religions*, 478.

2. Melton, *Melton's Encyclopedia of American Religions*, 478.

3. Melton, *Melton's Encyclopedia of American Religions*, 479.

4. Melton, *Melton's Encyclopedia of American Religions*, 511.

5. Melton, *Melton's Encyclopedia of American Religions*, 478–79, 511. For additional information about the Churches of Christ, see Frank S. Mead, *Handbook of Denominations in the United States*, 7th ed. (Nashville, TN: Abingdon, 1980), 100–102. Additionally, to find more data on the Churches of Christ in Alabama, see

"U.S. Congregational Membership Reports," Association of Religion Data Archives; "U.S. State Maps," Association of Religion Data Archives.

6. For more information, see Melton, *Melton's Encyclopedia of American Religions*, 635–39 and 644–45; Daniel Robertson and Tyler Bowles, "The Economics of Geographical Ward Boundaries in the LDS Church," *Journal of the Utah Academy of Sciences, Arts & Letters* 87 (2010). For more data on the Church of Jesus Christ of Latter-day Saints in Alabama, see "U.S. Congregational Membership Reports," Association of Religion Data Archives; "U.S. State Maps," Association of Religion Data Archives.

7. For information about the distinctiveness of the Churches of Christ and the Church of Jesus Christ of Latter-day Saints, as well as the tight-knit relationships among attenders of distinctive, strict, and theologically exclusive religious groups, see Laurence Iannaccone, "Why Strict Churches Are Strong," *American Journal of Sociology* 99, no. 5 (1994); Rodney Stark and Roger Finke, *Acts of Faith: Explaining the Human Side of Religion* (Berkeley, CA: University of California Press, 2000), 142–45; Christopher P. Scheitle and Amy Adamczyk, "It Takes Two: The Interplay of Individual and Group Theology on Social Embeddedness," *Journal for the Scientific Study of Religion* 48, no. 1 (2009); and Robert D. Putnam and David E. Campbell, *American Grace: How Religion Divides and Unites Us* (New York: Simon & Schuster, 2010), 536–39. For a rationale related to restoration, see McClure, "Congregations of a Feather," 574–75.

8. "Types of Biblical Hermeneutics," Britannica, accessed March 18, 2022, https://www.britannica.com/topic/biblical-literature/Types-of-biblical-hermeneutics#ref598267.

9. Gargiulo and Benassi, "Trapped in Your Own Net?" 193.

10. Ronald S. Burt, "Structural Holes versus Network Closure as Social Capital," in *Social Capital: Theory and Research*, eds. Nan Lin, Karen Cook, and Ronald S. Burt (New York: Taylor & Francis, 2001), 37–38, 48.

11. For research on relational constraints among individuals and in organizational settings, see Gargiulo and Benassi, "Trapped in Your Own Net?" 186; Kossinets and Watts, "Origins of Homophily in an Evolving Social Network," 436.

12. For an overview of research on intergroup contact, see Miles Hewstone and Hermann Swart, "Fifty-Odd Years of Inter-Group Contact: From Hypothesis to Integrated Theory," *British Journal of Social Psychology* 50 (2011).

CHAPTER 4

1. Granovetter, "The Strength of Weak Ties"; Granovetter, "The Strength of Weak Ties: A Network Theory Revisited."

2. For research on how congregations are more likely to have relationships within their religious groups, see McClure, "Congregations of a Feather." For research about how relationships that bridge across differences impact the spread of information and the effectiveness of collaborations, see Granovetter, "The Strength of Weak Ties"; Granovetter, "The Strength of Weak Ties: A Network Theory Revisited"; and Atouba and Shumate, "International Nonprofit Collaboration," 603.

3. Ammerman, *Pillars of Faith*, 111–12, 177–78. The quote is on p. 177.

4. "Who We Are," Greater Birmingham Ministries, accessed March 31, 2023, https://gbm.org/who-we-are/.

5. For research on relationships that bridge across differences and information diffusion, see Granovetter, "The Strength of Weak Ties"; Granovetter, "The Strength of Weak Ties: A Network Theory Revisited."

6. For research on diversity of relationships and the effectiveness of collaborations across nongovernmental organizations, see Atouba and Shumate, "International Nonprofit Collaboration," 603.

7. See more information on ARC in chapter 2 and at "About," Association of Related Churches.

8. 1 Corinthians 10:31 (NKJV).

9. According to this Muslim leader, all but one of the books were approved for use in schools, and one was "banned for a different reason."

10. "Faith in Action Alabama," Faith in Action, accessed March 10, 2022, https://faithinaction.org/federation/faith-in-action-alabama/.

11. If you're interested in learning more about community organizing, see Skjegstad, *7 Creative Models for Community Ministry*, 95–108.

12. Granovetter, "The Strength of Weak Ties: A Network Theory Revisited," 201.

CHAPTER 5

1. For more information about racial homophily among central Alabama congregations, see McClure, "Congregations of a Feather." Also see McPherson, Smith-Lovin, and Cook, "Birds of a Feather," 420–22, for more information about racial homophily among individuals, in classrooms, and in work settings; Emerson and Smith, *Divided by Faith*, and Chaves, *American Religion*, 24–28, for information about racial segregation in congregations. For more information about racial residential segregation, see Tracy Hadden Loh, Christopher Coes, and Becca Buthe, "Separate and Unequal: Persistent Residential Segregation Is Sustaining Racial and Economic Injustice in the U.S.," *The Brookings Institution*, published December 16, 2020, https://www.brookings.edu/essay/trend-1-separate-and-unequal-neighborhoods-are-sustaining-racial-and-economic-injustice-in-the-us/; William H. Frey, "Black-White Segregation Edges Downward Since 2000, Census Shows," *The Brookings Institution*, published December 17, 2018, https://www.brookings.edu/blog/the-avenue/2018/12/17/black-white-segregation-edges-downward-since-2000-census-shows/.

2. For congregations that participated in my 2017–2018 survey, 14% are in religious groups where 100% of the congregations are predominantly non-Hispanic white, 46% are in religious groups where at least 80% but not 100% of congregations are predominantly non-Hispanic white, and 9% are in religious groups where all congregations are predominantly African American. For information about the racial compositions of U.S. religious groups, see Lipka, "The Most and Least Racially Diverse U.S. Religious Groups."

3. See McClure, "Congregations of a Feather," for research on geographic homophily among congregations. The Alabama Constitution, which was adopted in 1901

and has been amended over 700 times, includes language requiring racial segregation in schools and poll taxes for voting. Alabama voters just voted to remove the racist language and laws in November 2022. See "Alabama Constitution of 1901," Alabama Department of Archives and History, accessed November 1, 2022, https://digital.archives.alabama.gov/digital/collection/constitutions/id/111/; Kim Chandler, "Alabama Seeks to Purge Racist Language from Constitution," *Associated Press*, November 3, 2021, https://apnews.com/article/alabama-race-and-ethnicity-racial-injustice-constitutions-constitutional-amendments-78c7dedd169e66e1accc65f440f88fff; "Alabama Constitution," Justia, accessed November 1, 2022, https://law.justia.com/constitution/alabama/; Johnn H. Glenn, "Election Results: Alabama Voters Approve New Constitution, 10 Amendments on Ballot," *FOX54*, November 9, 2022, https://www.rocketcitynow.com/article/news/local/alabama-constitution-change-2022-midterm-elections/525-8c6e1529-28e5-4dd8-b538-c8c2956bfa74. For the impact of racial residential segregation on educational inequality, see Equal Justice Initiative, "School Segregation in Alabama," published February 28, 2019, https://eji.org/news/history-racial-injustice-school-segregation-in-alabama/. For racial residential segregation in Birmingham, see Bobby M. Wilson, "Racial Segregation Trends in Birmingham, Alabama," *Southeastern Geographer* 25, no. 1 (1985); Frey, "Black-White Segregation Edges Downward Since 2000."

4. For research on Evangelical and Black Protestants, see Roger Finke and Rodney Stark, *The Churching of America 1776–2005: Winners and Losers in our Religious Economy* (New Brunswick, NJ: Rutgers University Press, 2005); Christian Smith, *American Evangelicalism: Embattled and Thriving* (Chicago, IL: University of Chicago Press, 1998); Emerson and Smith, *Divided by Faith*; C. Eric Lincoln and Lawrence H. Mamiya, *The Black Church in the African American Experience* (Durham, NC: Duke University Press, 1990); E. Franklin Frazier, *The Negro Church in America* (New York: Schocken Books, 1974 [1963]); Jennifer M. McClure, "Religious Tradition and Involvement in Congregational Activities That Focus on the Community," *Interdisciplinary Journal of Research on Religion* 10, no. 8 (2014); Kraig Beyerlein and John R. Hipp, "From Pews to Participation: The Effect of Congregational Activity and Context on Bridging Civic Engagement," *Social Problems* 53, no. 1 (2006). The quote "that Christ died " is from Emerson and Smith, *Divided by Faith*, 3.

5. Brian Steensland et al., "The Measure of American Religion: Toward Improving the State of the Art," *Social Forces* 79, no. 1 (2000); Justin Nortey, "Most White Americans Who Regularly Attend Worship Services Voted for Trump in 2020," Pew Research Center, published March 22, 2022, https://www.pewresearch.org/fact-tank/2021/08/30/most-white-americans-who-regularly-attend-worship-services-voted-for-trump in-2020/; Pew Research Center, "Race in America 2019," published April 9, 2019, https://www.pewresearch.org/social-trends/2019/04/09/race-in-america-2019/; Engy Abdelkader, "When It Comes to Religion and Politics, Race Trumps," Berkley Center for Religion, Peace and World Affairs, published May 24, 2021, https://berkleycenter.georgetown.edu/responses/when-it-comes-to-religion-and-politics race-trumps.

6. Michael Ollove and Christine Vestal, "COVID-19 Is Crushing Black Communities. Some States Are Paying Attention," *Pew Trust Magazine*, May 27,

2020, https://www.pewtrusts.org/en/research-and-analysis/blogs/stateline/2020/05/27
/covid-19-is-crushing-black-communities-some-states-are-paying-attention; Courtney Johnson and Cary Funk, "Black Americans Stand out for Their Concern
about COVID-19; 61% Say They Plan to Get Vaccinated or Already Have," Pew
Research Center, published March 9, 2021, https://www.pewresearch.org/fact-tank
/2021/03/09/black-americans-stand-out-for-their-concern-about-covid-19-61-say
-they-plan-to-get-vaccinated-or-already-have/; Adelle M. Banks, "'COVID Has
Been Harder on Us': Some Black Churches Remain Hesitant to Reopen," *Religion
News Service*, October 4, 2021, https://religionnews.com/2021/10/04/covid-has-been
-harder-on-us-some-black-churches-remain-hesitant-to-reopen/; Pew Research Center, "Health Concerns from COVID-19 Much Higher Among Hispanics and Blacks
Than Whites," published April 24, 2020, https://www.pewresearch.org/politics/2020
/04/14/health-concerns-from-covid-19-much-higher-among-hispanics-and-blacks
-than-whites/; Justin Nortey, "More Houses of Worship Are Returning to Normal
Operations, But In-Person Attendance Is Unchanged Since Fall," Pew Research
Center, published March 22, 2022, https://www.pewresearch.org/fact-tank/2022
/03/22/more-houses-of-worship-are-returning-to-normal-operations-but-in-person
-attendance-is-unchanged-since-fall/.

7. See McPherson, Smith-Lovin, and Cook, "Birds of a Feather," 420–22, for
more information about racial homophily among individuals and Emerson and
Smith, *Divided by Faith*, 135–51, for dynamics contributing to racial segregation in
congregations.

8. Pew Research Center, "On Views of Race and Inequality, Blacks and Whites
Are Worlds Apart," published June 27, 2016, https://www.pewresearch.org/social
-trends/2016/06/27/on-views-of-race-and-inequality-blacks-and-whites-are-worlds
-apart/. The quote "In providing a structured" comes from Frazier, *The Negro Church
in America*, 50–51.

9. See: Robert D. Putnam, *Bowling Alone: The Collapse and Revival of American
Community* (New York: Simon & Schuster, 2000), 22–23, for a description of bond-
ing social capital in homogeneous social circles; Burt, "Structural Holes versus Network Closure as Social Capital," for trust and support within tight-knit social groups;
Jennifer M. McClure, "Homophily and Social Capital in a Network of Religious Congregations," *Religions* 12, no. 8 (2021), for information about racially homogeneous
relationships and tight-knit networks in this study's network. The information about
relational constraints and the quote "constrained by whom" are from Kossinets and
Watts, "Origins of Homophily in an Evolving Social Network," 436.

10. For research on inter-group contact, see Gordon W. Allport, *The Nature of
Prejudice* (Reading, MA: Addison-Wesley Publishing Company, 1954), 261–82;
Hewstone and Swart, "Fifty-Odd Years of Inter-Group Contact."

CHAPTER 6

1. For research on situations in which religion promotes racial division and injustice, see Emerson and Smith, *Divided by Faith*; Whitehead and Perry, *Taking America*

Back for God. For research on intergroup contact, see Allport, *The Nature of Prejudice*, 261–82; Hewstone and Swart, "Fifty-Odd Years of Inter-Group Contact." For information about racial reconciliation and racial justice efforts between congregations, see Adelle M. Banks, "Can Churches' Focus on Race Move from Reconciliation to Justice?" *Religion News Service*, July 29, 2020, https://religionnews.com/2020/07/29/can-churches-focus-on-race-move-from-reconciliation-to-justice/.

2. For research on racial homophily among individuals, see McPherson, Smith-Lovin, and Cook, "Birds of a Feather." For research on racial homogeneity within congregations, see Emerson and Smith, *Divided by Faith*. For research on racial homophily in this network of congregations, see McClure, "Congregations of a Feather."

3. "About," Mission Reconcile, accessed March 31, 2022, https://iamareconciler.org/about/.

4. Ammerman, *Pillars of Faith*, 111–12, 177–78.

5. For research on relationships that bridge across differences and information diffusion, see Granovetter, "The Strength of Weak Ties"; Granovetter, "The Strength of Weak Ties: A Network Theory Revisited."

6. Audra D. S. Burch, "Birmingham Mayor Orders Removal of Confederate Monument in Public Park," *New York Times*, June 2, 2020, https://www.nytimes.com/2020/06/02/us/george-floyd-birmingham-confederate-statue.html; Malique Rankin, "One Year Later: Birmingham Riots, Confederate Monument Removed from Linn Park," *CBS42*, June 1, 2021, https://www.cbs42.com/news/one-year-later-birmingham-riots-confederate-monument-removed-from-linn-park/; and Brakkton Booker, "Confederate Monument Law Upheld by Alabama Supreme Court," *NPR*, November 27, 2019, https://www.npr.org/2019/11/27/783376085/confederate-monument-law-upheld-by-alabama-supreme-court.

7. For research on diversity of relationships and the effectiveness of collaborations across nongovernmental organizations, see Atouba and Shumate, "International Nonprofit Collaboration," 603.

8. For more information about the history of Red Mountain, see Carla Jean Whitley, "Red Mountain: The Past, Present and Future of Birmingham's Foundation," *AL.com*, January 2, 2015, https://www.al.com/bhammag/2015/01/red_mountain_the_foundation_of.html. To explore how communities are segregated in relation to Red Mountain, please search for Birmingham, AL, using the Community Profile Builder at "Community GIS Maps and Profile Reports," Association of Religion Data Archives, accessed November 8, 2022, https://thearda.com/us-religion/community-profiles/build-a-profile-of-your-community.

9. "About (&)," And Campaign, accessed March 31, 2022, https://www.andcampaign.org/about.

10. Ryan Kuja, "6 Harmful Consequences of the White Savior Complex," *Sojourners*, July 24, 2019, https://sojo.net/articles/6-harmful-consequences-white-savior-complex.

11. For research on how "members of disadvantaged groups are more likely to anticipate prejudice and discrimination against them from members of dominant groups"

in intergroup contact, see Hewstone and Swart, "Fifty-Odd Years of Inter-Group Contact," 375.

CHAPTER 7

1. This section draws heavily on content from McClure, "Connected and Fragmented."

2. For information about ministers' investments of time at their congregations and in their personal lives, see Carroll, *God's Potters*, 96–126. For information about how ministry impacts congregational ministers' personal lives, see Woolever and Bruce, *Leadership That Fits Your Church*, 55–56.

3. Proeschold-Bell and Byassee, *Faithful and Fractured*, 128.

4. Carroll, *God's Potters*, 212.

5. For more research on clergy health, see Woolever and Bruce, *Leadership That Fits Your Church*; Proeschold-Bell and Byassee, *Faithful and Fractured*.

6. For data on congregation sizes, see Mark Chaves and Shawna L. Anderson, "Changing American Congregations: Findings from the Third Wave of the National Congregations Study," *Journal for the Scientific Study of Religion* 53, no. 4 (2014): 682–84. For information on community service collaborations among congregations, see Ram Cnaan, *The Invisible Caring Hand: American Congregations and the Provision of Welfare* (New York: New York University Press, 2002), 70–75; Skjegstad, *7 Creative Models for Community Ministry*, 67–80; and Brad R. Fulton, "Network Ties and Organizational Action: Explaining Variation in Social Service Provision Patterns," *Management and Organizational Studies* 3, no. 3 (2016).

7. Skjegstad, *7 Creative Models for Community Ministry*, 67–80.

8. For more information on denominational gatherings for clergy, see Ammerman, *Pillars of Faith*, 109. For information on ministerial associations, see Ammerman, *Pillars of Faith*, 111–12, 177–78. For information on clergy peer groups, see Marler et al., *So Much Better*.

9. For information about the benefits of ministerial gatherings, see Ammerman, *Pillars of Faith*, 109–12; Marler et al., *So Much Better*, 7–9.

10. For more practical advice and for information about different ways to develop clergy peer groups, see Marler et al., *So Much Better*.

11. Mark Chaves, *Congregations in America* (Cambridge, MA: Harvard University Press, 2004), 232. In 1998, 65 percent of congregations hosted a minister from another congregation as a speaker.

12. McClure, "Congregations of a Feather," 576–77.

13. Granovetter, "The Strength of Weak Ties," 1361–62; Akinyemi, Harris, and Kawonga, "Innovation Diffusion"; and Proeschold-Bell and Byassee, *Faithful and Fractured*, 128.

14. See Granovetter, "The Strength of Weak Ties"; Granovetter, "The Strength of Weak Ties: A Network Theory Revisited"; and Atouba and Shumate, "International Nonprofit Collaboration." For research about how congregations whose relationships involve a relatively even mix of congregations from inside and outside of their

religious group have a wider reach within the network, see also McClure, "Homophily and Social Capital in a Network of Religious Congregations."

15. See Nagoski and Nagoski, *Burnout*, 214. "The cure for burnout is not 'self-care'; it is all of us caring for one another."

APPENDIX

1. McClure, "Connected and Fragmented," 5–13.

2. Melton, *Melton's Encyclopedia of American Religions*. A quote from the following source explains two changes from Melton's scheme: McClure, "Congregations of a Feather," 564. "This study's classification adds two categories. First, it differentiates Congregationalist (United Church of Christ, etc.) congregations from the Presbyterian/Reformed family. All of the non-Congregationalist Presbyterian/Reformed congregations in this study are from Presbyterian denominations (PC(USA), PCA, Cumberland Presbyterian, etc.), and no participants are from Reformed denominations (Reformed Church in America, Christian Reformed Church, etc.). This study differentiates Presbyterian and Congregationalist families due to differing polity styles and distinct family trees (Ammerman 2005:224; Melton 2009:241–244). Second, this study separates Restorationist congregations from the Baptist family due to distinct historical trees (Melton 2009:476, 479)."

3. The following article provides more information: McClure, "Congregations of a Feather," 564. "Four congregations with denominational affiliations were classified as having an unclear family because their denomination was not included in and could not easily be categorized in Melton's classification (2009). Using a variety of factors, I classified as many nondenominational congregations (N=82) as possible into Melton's scheme. Over half (N=43) were classified as Pentecostal due to indicating that speaking in tongues was typically part of their worship services and/or that 'charismatic' described the congregation's identity. Fourteen nondenominational congregations were classified as Baptist. Almost all included 'Baptist' in the congregation's name; a few that did not include 'Baptist' in their name strongly emphasized the priesthood of believers in the statement of faith posted on their website (Flynt 1998:168). One nondenominational congregation was classified as Methodist/Pietist because it included 'Methodist' in its name. Twelve nondenominational Church of Christ congregations were classified as Restorationist. The twelve remaining nondenominational congregations were considered to have an 'unclear' family."

4. In Michael O. Emerson and Karen Chai Kim, "Multiracial Congregations: An Analysis of Their Development and a Typology," 217, multiracial congregations are defined as "less than 80% of the members shar[ing] the same racial background."

5. Steensland et al., "The Measure of American Religion."

6. According to McClure, "Congregations of a Feather," 565, the community types are "based on the National Center for Education Statistics' framework for classifying communities (Geverdt 2015). The location types for each congregation were ascertained through geolocating each congregation in GIS and matching each location with 2017 NCES locale data." According to Jennifer M. McClure, "Is Together Better?

Investigating the Relationship between Network Dynamics and Congregations' Vitality and Sustainability," *Review of Religious Research* 64, no. 3 (2022): 463, the racial and economic characteristics of households "for each congregation's Census tract [were] ascertained through geolocating each congregation in GIS and matching each location with 2013–2017 American Community Survey data."

7. There is a strong, negative correlation between the percentage of residents in a congregation's Census tract who are non-Hispanic white and the percentage of residents in a congregation's Census tract who are African American (r=-0.98; p<0.001; N=438). For more information about how the poverty level is determined, see U.S. Department of Health and Human Services, "2018 Poverty Guidelines," Office of the Assistant Secretary for Planning and Evaluation, https://aspe.hhs.gov/topics/poverty -economic-mobility/poverty-guidelines/prior-hhs-poverty-guidelines-federal-register -references/2018-poverty-guidelines. Also, median, not average, household income is used because high income values can result in an average household income that is higher than the typical income.

8. McClure, "Connected and Fragmented," 13–15.

9. To learn more about the procedure for creating the clusters, see Clauset, Newman, and Moore, "Finding Community Structure in Very Large Networks."

10. Rotolo and McPherson, "The System of Occupations," 1101.

11. A definition of a tie can be found in Stanley Wasserman and Katherine Faust, *Social Network Analysis*: *Methods and Applications* (Cambridge, MA: Harvard University Press, 1994), 18. For the definition for an alter, see Christina Prell, *Social Network Analysis: History, Theory and Methodology* (Thousand Oaks, CA: Sage Publications, 2012), 8–9. See McPherson, Smith-Lovin, and Cook, "Birds of a Feather," for an overview of research on homophily. Research on homophily in this network of congregations is available in McClure, "Congregations of a Feather."

12. A previous research note explains the impact of only measuring homophily from alters that participated in the survey: McClure, "Congregations of a Feather," 568–69. "There are two additional factors that impact the analyses. First, congregations without any participating alters are excluded from the regression analyses, because proportions and averages [for measuring homophily] cannot be computed from zero alters. Of the 438 participating congregations, 31 (7.1%) did not have any alters that participated in the study. A supplemental analysis sought to examine the extent to which congregational characteristics predicted whether or not congregations had alters that participated. Analyses examined a variety of bivariate relationships, but only one, which involved the main minister's tenure at the congregation, was significant at p<0.05; the percentages of congregations that do not have alters who participated in the study, by the main minister's tenure at the congregation, are 8.6% for under five years, 1.2% for five to nine years, 6.1% for 10–19 years, and 13.1% for 20 or more years. Second, many congregations mentioned alters that did not ultimately participate in the study. On average, just over 60% of the alters mentioned by each participant actually participated, and there is significant variation among participants in the percentage of alters that participated (mean=62.1%; SD=25.6%). This study's focus on relational ties in which both congregations participated in the study results

in a bias in this research note's analyses, where the quality of analysis varies due to differences in the percentage of participating alters mentioned by each participant. In other words, this analysis can more adequately gauge the homophily of a congregation where 90% of its alters participated than a congregation where 30% of its alters participated. An additional supplemental analysis sought to examine how the percentage of participating alters varies by congregational characteristics. The following characteristics correspond with congregations where, on average, at least 70% of their alters participated in the study (leading to more complete data on their similarity to or difference from alters): Roman Catholic and other (not Protestant or Roman Catholic) traditions; Anglican, Latter-day Saint, and Roman Catholic families; multisite; average weekly attendance of 500 or more; budget of more than $1,000,000. The following characteristics correspond with congregations where, on average, about 55% or less of their alters participated in the study (leading to more incomplete data on their similarity to or difference from alters): no denominational affiliation; Black Protestant tradition; Holiness, Pentecostal, and Restorationist families; African American racial composition; certificate or bachelor-level theological education; no budget."

References

Abdelkader, Engy. "When It Comes to Religion and Politics, Race Trumps." Berkley Center for Religion, Peace and World Affairs. Published May 24, 2021. https://berkleycenter.georgetown.edu/responses/when-it-comes-to-religion-and-politics-race-trumps.

Ahuja, Gautam. "Collaboration Networks, Structural Holes, and Innovation: A Longitudinal Study." *Administrative Science Quarterly* 45 (2000): 425–55.

Akinyemi, Oluwaseun, Bronwyn Harris, and Mary Kawonga. "Innovation Diffusion: How Homogeneous Networks Influence the Uptake of Community-Based Injectable Contraceptives." BMC Public Health 19 (2019): 1520–31.

Alabama Department of Archives and History. "Alabama Constitution of 1901." Accessed November 1, 2022. https://digital.archives.alabama.gov/digital/collection/constitutions/id/111/.

Allport, Gordon W. *The Nature of Prejudice*. Reading, MA: Addison-Wesley, 1954.

American Fellowship of Cowboy Churches. "American Fellowship of Cowboy Churches." Accessed November 1, 2022. https://americanfcc.org/.

Ammerman, Nancy T. *Congregation and Community*. New Brunswick, NJ: Rutgers University Press, 1997.

———. *Pillars of Faith: American Congregations and Their Partners*. Berkeley, CA: University of California Press, 2005.

And Campaign. "About (&)." Accessed March 31, 2022. https://www.andcampaign.org/about.

Association of Related Churches. "About." Accessed January 28, 2022. https://www.arcchurches.com/about/.

Association of Religion Data Archives. "Community GIS Maps and Profile Reports." Accessed November 8, 2022. https://thearda.com/us-religion/community-profiles/build-a-profile-of-your-community.

———. "U.S. Congregational Membership Reports." Accessed November 8, 2022. https://thearda.com/us-religion/census/congregational-membership.

———. "U.S. State Maps." Accessed November 8, 2022. https://thearda.com/us-religion/maps/us-state-maps.

Atouba, Yannick C., and Michelle Shumate. "International Nonprofit Collaboration: Examining the Role of Homophily." *Nonprofit and Voluntary Sector Quarterly* 44, no. 3 (2015): 587–608.

Banks, Adelle M. "Amid COVID-19, Most Churches Provide Hybrid Worship, Half Stopped Picnics." *Religion News Service*, November 10, 2021. https://religionnews.com/2021/11/10/amid-covid-19-most-churches-provide-hybrid-worship-half-stopped-picnics/.

———. "Can Churches' Focus on Race Move from Reconciliation to Justice?" Religion News Service, July 29, 2020.https://religionnews.com/2020/07/29/can-churches-focus-on-race-move-from-reconciliation-to-justice/.

———. "Churches' Ministry to Those Hurt by the Pandemic Shows 'Monumental' Growth, Study Says." *Religion News Service*, December 21, 2021.https://religionnews.com/2021/12/21/churches-adapt-social-ministries-even-as-they-lose-members-to-the-pandemic/.

———. "'COVID Has Been Harder on Us': Some Black Churches Remain Hesitant to Reopen." *Religion News Service*, October 4, 2021. https://religionnews.com/2021/10/04/covid-has-been-harder-on-us-some-black-churches-remain-hesitant-to-reopen/.

Barna Group. "38% of U.S. Pastors Have Thought About Quitting Full-Time Ministry in the Past Year." Updated 2021. https://www.barna.com/research/pastors-well-being/.

Bergstresser, Jack. "Iron and Steel Production in Birmingham." Encyclopedia of Alabama. Accessed November 4, 2022. http://encyclopediaofalabama.org/Article/h-1638#:~:text=In%20the%20decades%20after%20the,in%20the%20southern%20United%20States.

Beyerlein, Kraig, and John R. Hipp. "From Pews to Participation: The Effect of Congregational Activity and Context on Bridging Civic Engagement." Social Problems 53, no. 1 (2006): 97–117.

Booker, Brakkton. "Confederate Monument Law Upheld by Alabama Supreme Court." *NPR*, November 27, 2019. https://www.npr.org/2019/11/27/783376085/confederate-monument-law-upheld-by-alabama-supreme-court.

Boorstein, Michelle. "The First Christmas as a Layperson: Burned Out by the Pandemic, Many Clergy Quit in the Past Year." *Washington Post*, December 24, 2021. https://www.washingtonpost.com/religion/2021/12/24/christmas-covid-pandemic-clergy-quit/.

Britannica. "Types of Biblical Hermeneutics." Accessed March 18, 2022. https://www.britannica.com/topic/biblical-literature/Types-of-biblical-hermeneutics#ref598267.

Brown, Matthew. "Pew Analysis: Sermons Turned to Political Messaging in 2020 amid Election, Protests, COVID-19." USA Today, July 11, 2021. https://www.usatoday.com/story/news/politics/2021/07/11/pew-analysis-sermons-turned-political-2020-amid-covid-election/7930097002/.

Burch, Audra D. S. "Birmingham Mayor Orders Removal of Confederate Monument in Public Park." *New York Times*, June 2, 2020. https://www.nytimes.com/2020/06/02/us/george-floyd-birmingham-confederate-statue.html.

Burt, Ronald S. "Structural Holes versus Network Closure as Social Capital." In *Social Capital: Theory and Research*, edited by Nan Lin, Karen Cook, and Ronald S. Burt, 31–56. New York: Taylor & Francis, 2001.

Carroll, Jackson W. *God's Potters: Pastoral Leadership and the Shaping of Congregations*. Grand Rapids, MI: William B. Eerdmans Publishing, 2006.

Chandler, Kim. "Alabama Seeks to Purge Racist Language from Constitution." Associated Press, November 3, 2021. https://apnews.com/article/alabama -race-and-ethnicity-racial-injustice-constitutions-constitutional-amendments -78c7dedd169e66e1accc65f440f88fff.

Chaves, Mark. *American Religion: Contemporary Trends*. 2nd ed. Princeton, NJ: Princeton University Press, 2017.

———. *Congregations in America*. Cambridge, MA: Harvard University Press, 2004.

Chaves, Mark, and Shawna L. Anderson. "Changing American Congregations: Findings from the Third Wave of the National Congregations Study." *Journal for the Scientific Study of Religion* 53, no. 4 (2014): 676–86.

City-Data. "Birmingham: Economy." Accessed November 4, 2022. https://www.city -data.com/us-cities/The-South/Birmingham-Economy.html.

City of Tuscaloosa. "History of Tuscaloosa." Accessed November 4, 2022. https:// www.tuscaloosa.com/history.

Clauset, Aaron, M. E. J. Newman, and Cristopher Moore. "Finding Community Structure in Very Large Networks." *Physical Review E* 70, no. 6 (2004): 1–6.

Cnaan, Ram. *The Invisible Caring Hand: American Congregations and the Provision of Welfare*. New York: New York University Press, 2002.

Colurso, Mary. "James Beard Awards: 7 Birmingham Restaurants and Chefs Honored by 'Oscars of the Food World.'" *AL.com*, July 31, 2022. https://www.al.com/life /2022/07/james-beard-awards-7-birmingham-restaurants-and-chefs-honored-by- oscars-of-the-food-world.html.

Cormode, Scott. *The Innovative Church: How Leaders and Their Congregations Can Adapt in an Ever-Changing World*. Grand Rapids, MI: Baker Academic, 2020.

Creamer, John, Emily A. Shrider, Kalee Burns, and Frances Chen. *Poverty in the United States: 2021*. Washington, DC: U.S. Census Bureau, 2022. https://www .census.gov/content/dam/Census/library/publications/2022/demo/p60-277.pdf.

Dimock, Michael, and Richard Wike. "America Is Exceptional in Its Political Divide." *Pew Trust Magazine*, March 29, 2021. https://www.pewtrusts.org/en/trust /archive/winter-2021/america-is-exceptional-in-its-political-divide.

Elliott, Debbie. "'Day You'll Never Forget': Decade after Deadly Tuscaloosa Tornado, Recovery Is Uneven." *NPR*, April 27, 2021. https://www.npr.org/2021/04 /27/991277578/day-youll-never-forget-decade-after-deadly-tuscaloosa-tornado- recovery-is-uneven.

Emerson, Michael O., and Karen Chai Kim. "Multiracial Congregations: An Analysis of Their Development and a Typology." *Journal for the Scientific Study of Religion* 42, no. 2 (2003): 217–27.

Emerson, Michael O., and Christian Smith. *Divided by Faith: Evangelical Religion and the Problem of Race in America*. New York: Oxford University Press, 2000.

Episcopal Church. "Peace, The." An Episcopal Dictionary of the Church. Accessed January 28, 2022. https://www.episcopalchurch.org/glossary/peace-the/.

Equal Justice Initiative. "School Segregation in Alabama." Published February 28, 2019. https://eji.org/news/history-racial-injustice-school-segregation-in-alabama/.

Evans, Elizabeth E. "For Clergy, COVID-19 Has Brought Both Burnout and Breakthrough." *Religion News Service*, February 21, 2022. https://religionnews.com /2022/02/21/for-clergy-covid-19-has-brought-both-burnout-and-breakthrough/.

Fairchild, Mary. "How Does the Bible Define Discipleship?" Learn Religions. Updated December 11, 2019. https://www.learnreligions.com/discipleship-definition-4132340.

Faith in Action. "Faith in Action Alabama." Accessed March 10, 2022. https:// faithinaction.org/federation/faith-in-action-alabama/.

Felicetti, Elizabeth. "My Church Doesn't Know What to Do Anymore." *The Atlantic*, October 27, 2021. https://www.theatlantic.com/ideas/archive/2021/10/church -pandemic/620496/.

Finke, Roger, and Rodney Stark. *The Churching of America 1776–2005: Winners and Losers in Our Religious Economy*. New Brunswick, NJ: Rutgers University Press, 2005.

Flynt, Wayne. *Alabama Baptists: Southern Baptists in the Heart of Dixie*. Tuscaloosa, AL: University of Alabama Press, 1998.

Frazier, E. Franklin. *The Negro Church in America*. New York: Schocken Books, 1974 [1963].

Frey, William H. "Black-White Segregation Edges Downward since 2000, Census Shows." The Brookings Institution. Published December 17, 2018. https:// www.brookings.edu/blog/the-avenue/2018/12/17/black-white-segregation-edges-downward-since-2000-census-shows/.

Fulton, Brad R. "Network Ties and Organizational Action: Explaining Variation in Social Service Provision Patterns." *Management and Organizational Studies* 3, no. 3 (2016): 1–20.

Gargiulo, Martin, and Mario Benassi. "Trapped in Your Own Net? Network Cohesion, Structural Holes, and the Adaptation of Social Capital." *Organization Science* 11, no. 2 (2000): 183–96.

Gecewicz, Claire. "Few Americans Say Their House of Worship Is Open, But a Quarter Say Their Faith Has Grown amid Pandemic." Pew Research Center. Published April 30, 2020. https://www.pewresearch.org/fact-tank/2020/04/30/few -americans-say-their-house-of-worship-is-open-but-a-quarter-say-their-religious -faith-has-grown-amid-pandemic/.

Geverdt, Douglas E. *Education Demographic and Geographic Estimates Program (EDGE): Locale Boundaries User's Manual*. Washington, DC: National Center for Education Statistics, 2015. https://nces.ed.gov/programs/edge/docs/NCES_LOCA LE_USERSMANUAL_2016012.pdf.

Glenn, Johnn H. "Election Results: Alabama Voters Approve New Constitution, 10 Amendments on Ballot." *FOX54*, November 9, 2022. https://www.rocketcitynow .com/article/news/local/alabama-constitution-change-2022-midterm-elections/525-8c6e1529-28e5-4dd8-b538-c8c2956bfa74.

Gondal, Neha. "Inequality Preservation through Uneven Diffusion of Cultural Materials across Stratified Groups." *Social Forces* 93, no. 3 (2015): 1109–37.

Granovetter, Mark. "The Strength of Weak Ties." *American Journal of Sociology* 78, no. 6 (1973): 1360–80.

———. "The Strength of Weak Ties: A Network Theory Revisited." *Sociological Theory* 1 (1983): 201–33.

Greater Birmingham Ministries. "Who We Are." Accessed March 31, 2023. https://gbm.org/who-we-are/.

Hartford Institute for Religion Research. *Congregational Response to the Pandemic: Extraordinary Social Outreach in a Time of Crisis.* Hartford, CT: Hartford Institute for Religion Research, 2021. https://www.covidreligionresearch.org/wp-content/uploads/2021/12/Congregational-Response-to-the-Pandemic_Extraordinary-Social-Outreach-in-a-Time-of-Crisis_Dec-2021.pdf.

———. *Navigating the Pandemic: A First Look at Congregational Responses.* Hartford, CT: Hartford Institute for Religion Research, 2021. https://www.covidreligionresearch.org/wp-content/uploads/2021/11/Navigating-the-Pandemic_A-First-Look-at-Congregational-Responses_Nov-2021.pdf.

Hewstone, Miles, and Hermann Swart. "Fifty-Odd Years of Inter-Group Contact: From Hypothesis to Integrated Theory." *British Journal of Social Psychology* 50 (2011): 374–86.

House, James S., Debra Umberson, and Kark R. Landis. "Structures and Processes of Social Support." *Annual Review of Sociology* 14 (1988): 293–318.

Iannaccone, Laurence. "Why Strict Churches Are Strong." *American Journal of Sociology* 99, no. 5 (1994): 1118–1211.

Johnson, Courtney, and Cary Funk. "Black Americans Stand Out for Their Concern about COVID-19; 61% Say They Plan to Get Vaccinated or Already Have." Pew Research Center. Published March 9, 2021. https://www.pewresearch.org/fact-tank/2021/03/09/black-americans-stand-out-for-their-concern-about-covid-19_61_say-they-plan-to-get-vaccinated-or-already-have/.

Justia. "Alabama Constitution." Accessed November 1, 2022. https://law.justia.com/constitution/alabama/.

King, Martin Luther Jr. *Letter from Birmingham Jail.* London: Penguin, 2018.

Kossinets, Gueorgi, and Duncan J. Watts. "Origins of Homophily in an Evolving Social Network." *American Journal of Sociology* 115, no. 2 (2009). 405–50.

Krause, Neal, Christopher G. Ellison, Benjamin A. Shaw, John P. Marcum, and Jason D. Boardman. "Church-Based Social Support and Religious Coping." *Journal for the Scientific Study of Religion* 40, no. 4 (2001): 637–56.

Kuja, Ryan. "6 Harmful Consequences of the White Savior Complex." *Sojourners*, July 24, 2019. https://sojo.net/articles/6-harmful-consequences-white-savior-complex.

Langford, Catherine P. H., Juanita Bowsher, Joseph P. Maloney, and Patricia P. Lillis. "Social Support: A Conceptual Analysis." *Journal of Advanced Nursing* 25 (1997). 95–100.

Library of Congress. "Governor George Wallace Attempting to Block Integration at the University of Alabama." Prints and Photographs Online Catalog. Accessed November 7, 2022. https://www.loc.gov/pictures/item/2003688161/.

Lincoln, C. Eric, and Lawrence H. Mamiya. *The Black Church in the African American Experience*. Durham, NC: Duke University Press, 1990.

Lipka, Michael. "The Most and Least Racially Diverse U.S. Religious Groups." Pew Research Center. Published July 27, 2015. https://www.pewresearch.org/fact-tank/2015/07/27/the-most-and-least-racially-diverse-u-s-religious-groups/.

Loh, Tracy Hadden, Christopher Coes, and Becca Buthe. "Separate and Unequal: Persistent Residential Segregation Is Sustaining Racial and Economic Injustice in the U.S." *The* Brookings Institution. Published December 16, 2020. https://www.brookings.edu/essay/trend-1-separate-and-unequal-neighborhoods-are-sustaining-racial-and-economic-injustice-in-the-us/.

Marler, Penny Long, D. Bruce Roberts, Janet Maykus, James Bowers, Larry Dill, Brenda K. Harewood, Richard Hester, Sheila Kirton-Robbins, Marianne LaBarre, Lis Van Harten, and Kelli Walker-Jones. *So Much Better: How Thousands of Pastors Help Each Other Thrive*. St. Louis, MO: Chalice Press, 2013.

McClure, Jennifer M. "Congregations of a Feather? Exploring Homophily in a Network of Religious Congregations." *Review of Religious Research* 63, no. 4 (2021): 559–82. https://doi.org/10.1007/s13644-021-00449-y.

———. "Connected and Fragmented: Introducing a Social Network Study of Religious Congregations." *Interdisciplinary Journal of Research on Religion* 16, no. 4 (2020): 1–33.

———. "Homophily and Social Capital in a Network of Religious Congregations." *Religions* 12, no. 8 (2021): 653. https://doi.org/10.3390/rel12080653.

———. "Is Together Better? Investigating the Relationship between Network Dynamics and Congregations' Vitality and Sustainability." *Review of Religious Research* 64, no. 3 (2022): 451–74. https://doi.org/10.1007/s13644-022-00496-z.

———. "Religious Tradition and Involvement in Congregational Activities That Focus on the Community." *Interdisciplinary Journal of Research on Religion* 10, no. 8 (2014): 1–30.

McPherson, Miller, Lynn Smith-Lovin, and James M. Cook. "Birds of a Feather: Homophily in Social Networks." *Annual Review of Sociology* 27 (2001): 415–44.

Mead, Frank S. *Handbook of Denominations in the United States*. 7th ed. Nashville, TN: Abingdon, 1980.

Melton, J. Gordon. *Melton's Encyclopedia of American Religions*. 8th ed. Detroit, MI: Gale, 2009.

Merton, Thomas. *No Man Is an Island*. New York: Harcourt, 1955.

Miles, Kyra. "The World Games Kicks Off in Birmingham." *WBHM*, July 7, 2022. https://wbhm.org/2022/the-world-games-kicks-off-in-birmingham/.

Mission Reconcile. "About." Accessed March 31, 2023. https://iamareconciler.org/about/.

Nagoski, Emily, and Amelia Nagoski. *Burnout: The Secret to Unlocking the Stress Cycle*. New York: Ballantine Books, 2019.

———. "Episode 31: Social Support." *Feminist Survival Project 2020*, May 17, 2020. Podcast, MP3 audio, 39:36. https://www.feministsurvivalproject.com/episodes/episode-31-social-support.

National Aeronautics and Space Administration. "Tuscaloosa Tornado Track Fades." NASA Earth Observatory. Accessed November 7, 2022. https://earthobservatory .nasa.gov /images/87972/tuscaloosa-tornado-track-fades.

National Park Service. "16th Street Baptist Church Bombing (1963)." Accessed November 4, 2022. https://www.nps.gov/articles/16thstreetbaptist.htm.

Nortey, Justin. "More Houses of Worship Are Returning to Normal Operations, But In-Person Attendance Is Unchanged Since Fall." Pew Research Center. Published March 22, 2022. https://www.pewresearch.org/fact-tank/2022/03/22/more-houses -of-worship-are-returning-to-normal-operations-but-in-person-attendance-is -unchanged-since-fall/.

———. "Most White Americans Who Regularly Attend Worship Services Voted for Trump in 2020." Pew Research Center. Published August 30, 2021. https://www.pewresearch.org/fact-tank/2021/08/30/most-white-americans- who-regularly-attend-worship-services-voted-for-trump-in-2020/.

Ollove, Michael, and Christine Vestal. "COVID-19 Is Crushing Black Communities. Some States Are Paying Attention." *Pew Trust Magazine*, May 27, 2020. https:// www.pewtrusts.org/en/research-and-analysis/blogs/stateline/2020/05/27/covid-19 -is-crushing-black-communities-some-states-are-paying-attention.

Othering and Belonging Institute. "Most to Least Segregated Cities." Accessed November 4, 2022. https://belonging.berkeley.edu/most-least-segregated-cities.

Pew Research Center. "The Generation Gap in American Politics." Published March 1, 2018. https://www.pewresearch.org/politics/2018/03/01/the-generation-gap-in -american-politics/.

———. "Health Concerns from COVID-19 Much Higher Among Hispanics and Blacks Than Whites." Published April 24, 2020. https://www.pewresearch.org/ politics /2020/04/14/health-concerns-from-covid-19-much-higher-among-hispan- ics-and-blacks-than-whites/.

———. "In U.S., Decline of Christianity Continues at Rapid Pace." Published October 17, 2019. https://www.pewforum.org/2019/10/17/in-u-s-decline-of -christianity-continues-at-rapid-pace/.

———. "'Nones' on the Rise." Published October 9, 2012. https://www.pewforum .org/2012/10/09/nones-on-the-rise/.

———. "On Views of Race and Inequality, Blacks and Whites Are Worlds Apart." Published June 27, 2016. https://www.pewresearch.org/social-trends/2016/06/27/ on-views-of-race-and-inequality-blacks-and-whites-are-worlds-apart/.

———. "Race in America 2019." Published April 9, 2019. https://www.pewresearch .org/social-trends/2019/04/09/race-in-america-2019/.

———. "Voters' Attitudes About Race and Gender Are Even More Divided Than in 2016." Published September 10, 2020. https://www.pewresearch.org/politics /2020/09/10/voters-attitudes-about-race-and-gender-are-even-more-divided-than -in-2016/.

Politico. "Alabama Presidential Results." Accessed November 4, 2022. https://www .politico.com/2020-election/results/alabama/.

Powell, Kara, Jake Mulder, and Brad Griffin. *Growing Young: 6 Essential Strategies to Help Young People Discover and Love Your Church*. Grand Rapids, MI: Baker Books, 2016.

Prell, Christina. *Social Network Analysis: History, Theory and Methodology*. Thousand Oaks, CA: Sage Publications, 2012.

Proeschold-Bell, Rae Jean, and Jason Byassee. *Faithful and Fractured: Responding to the Clergy Health Crisis*. Grand Rapids, MI: Baker Academic, 2018.

Putnam, Robert D. *Bowling Alone: The Collapse and Revival of American Community*. New York: Simon & Schuster, 2000.

Putnam, Robert D., and David E. Campbell. *American Grace: How Religion Divides and Unites Us*. New York: Simon & Schuster, 2010.

Rankin, Malique. "One Year Later: Birmingham Riots, Confederate Monument Removed from Linn Park." *CBS42*, June 1, 2021. https://www.cbs42.com/news/one-year-later-birmingham-riots-confederate-monument-removed-from-linn-park/.

Robertson, Daniel, and Tyler Bowles. "The Economics of Geographical Ward Boundaries in the LDS Church." *Journal of the Utah Academy of Sciences, Arts & Letters* 87 (2010): 317–35.

Rotolo, Thomas, and J. Miller McPherson. "The System of Occupations: Modeling Occupations in Sociodemographic Space." *Social Forces* 79, no. 3 (2001): 1095–1130.

Scheitle, Christopher P., and Amy Adamczyk. "It Takes Two: The Interplay of Individual and Group Theology on Social Embeddedness." *Journal for the Scientific Study of Religion* 48, no. 1 (2009): 16–29.

Serve Day. "Serve." Accessed March 7, 2022. https://serveday.com/.

Shepard, Bob. "UAB Hospital Now Eighth-Largest in the Nation." *UAB News*, December 7, 2021. https://www.uab.edu/news/health/item/12492-uab-hospital-now-eighth-largest-in-the-nation.

Shimron, Yonat. "Study: Attendance Hemorrhaging at Small and Midsize U.S. Congregations." *Religion News Service*, October 14, 2021. https://religionnews.com/2021/10/14/study-attendance-at-small-and-midsize-us-congregations-is-hemorrhaging/.

Shipilov, Andrew V., and Stan Xiao Li. "Can You Have Your Cake and Eat It Too? Structural Holes' Influence on Status Accumulation and Market Performance in Collaborative Networks." *Administrative Science Quarterly* 53 (2008): 73–108.

Skjegstad, Joy F. *7 Creative Models for Community Ministry*. Valley Forge, PA: Judson Press, 2013.

Smietana, Bob. *Reorganized Religion: The Reshaping of the American Church and Why It Matters*. New York: Worthy Publishing, 2022.

Smith, Christian. *American Evangelicalism: Embattled and Thriving*. Chicago, IL: University of Chicago Press, 1998.

Smith, Gregory A. "About Three-in-Ten U.S. Adults Are Now Religiously Unaffiliated." Pew Research Center. Published December 14, 2021. https://www.pewresearch.org/religion/2021/12/14/about-three-in-ten-u-s-adults-are-now-religiously-unaffiliated/.

Smith, Jeffrey A., Miller McPherson, and Lynn Smith-Lovin. "Social Distance in the United States: Sex, Race, Religion, Age, and Education Homophily among Confidants, 1985 to 2004." *American Sociological Review* 79, no. 3 (2014): 432–56.

Soda, Giuseppe, Alessandro Usai, and Akbar Zaheer. "Network Memory: The Influence of Past and Current Networks on Performance." *The Academy of Management Journal* 47, no. 6 (2004): 893–906.

Southern Baptist Convention. "Baptist Faith and Message 2000." Accessed January 18, 2022. https://bfm.sbc.net/bfm2000/#xiv-cooperation.

Stark, Rodney, and Roger Finke. *Acts of Faith: Explaining the Human Side of Religion*. Berkeley, CA: University of California Press, 2000.

Steensland, Brian, Jerry Z. Park, Mark D. Regnerus, Lynn D. Robinson, W. Bradford Wilcox, and Robert D. Woodberry. "The Measure of American Religion: Toward Improving the State of the Art." *Social Forces* 79, no. 1 (2000): 291–318.

Steinke, Peter L. *Uproar: Calm Leadership in Anxious Times*. Lanham, MD: Rowman & Littlefield, 2019.

Taylor, Shelley E. "Social Support: A Review." In *The Oxford Handbook of Health Psychology*, edited by Howard S. Friedman, 189–214. New York: Oxford University Press, 2011.

Thumma, Scott. "Is a Great Resignation Brewing for Pastors?" *Religion News Service*, March 18, 2022. https://religionnews.com/2022/03/18/is-a-great-resignation-brewing-for-pastors/.

———. "The Pandemic Impact on Congregations: What Do We Know and What Still Needs to Be Learned?" Presentation at Lilly Endowment's Thriving Congregations Annual Gathering, Indianapolis, IN, October 10–12, 2022.

U.S. Census Bureau. "QuickFacts Alabama; United States." Accessed November 7, 2022. https://www.census.gov/quickfacts/fact/table/AL,US/PST045221.

U.S. Civil Rights Trail. "Birmingham Civil Rights Institute." Accessed November 4, 2022. https://civilrightstrail.com/attraction/birmingham-civil-rights-institute/.

U.S. Department of Health and Human Services. "2018 Poverty Guidelines." Office of the Assistant Secretary for Planning and Evaluation. Published 2018. https://aspe.hhs.gov/topics/poverty-economic-mobility/poverty-guidelines/prior-hhs-poverty-guidelines-federal-register-references/2018-poverty-guidelines.

U.S. News & World Report. "Education Rankings." Accessed November 4, 2022. https://www.usnews.com/news/best-states/rankings/education.

———. "Health Care Rankings." Accessed November 4, 2022. https://www.usnews.com/news/best-states/rankings/health-care.

———. "Public Health Rankings." Accessed November 4, 2022. https://www.usnews.com/news/best-states/rankings/health-care/public-health.

Wasserman, Stanley, and Katherine Faust. *Social Network Analysis: Methods and Applications*. Cambridge, MA: Harvard University Press, 1994.

Whitehead, Andrew L., and Samuel L. Perry. *Taking America Back for God: Christian Nationalism in the United States*. New York: Oxford University Press, 2020.

Whitley, Carla Jean. "Red Mountain: The Past, Present and Future of Birmingham's Foundation." *AL.com*, January 2, 2015. https://www.al.com/bhammag/2015/01/red_mountain_the_foundation_of.html.

Wilson, Bobby M. "Racial Segregation Trends in Birmingham, Alabama." *Southeastern Geographer* 25, no. 1 (1985): 30–43.

Woolever, Cynthia, and Deborah Bruce. *Leadership That Fits Your Church: What Kind of Pastor for What Kind of Congregation*. St. Louis, MO: Chalice Press, 2012.

Zaheer, Akbar, and Geoffrey G. Bell. "Benefiting from Network Position: Firm Capabilities, Structural Holes, and Performance." *Strategic Management Journal* 26, no. 9 (2005): 809–25.

Index

147

About the Author

Jennifer M. McClure Haraway is a sociologist of religion who studies local congregations. She is an associate professor of religion and sociology at Samford University in Birmingham, Alabama. She also develops congregational resources with the Association of Religion Data Archives and serves as the congregational research strategist at Samford's Center for Congregational Resources.